DAILY READINGS

Sri Swami Sivananda

Published by
THE DIVINE LIFE SOCIETY
P.O. SHIVANANDANAGAR—249 192
Distt. Tehri-Garhwal, Uttarakhand, Himalayas,
India

Price] 2009 [Rs. 70/-

First Edition:	1958
Second Edition:	1965
Third Edition:	2007
Fourth Edition:	2009

[1000 Copies]

©The Divine Life Trust Society

ISBN 81-7052-215-3

ES73

Published by Swami Vimalananda for
The Divine Life Society, Shivanandanagar, and printed by him
at the Yoga-Vedanta Forest Academy Press,
P.O. Shivanandanagar, Distt. Tehri-Garhwal, Uttarakhand,
Himalayas, India

SRI SWAMI SIVANANDA

Born on the 8th September, 1887, in the illustrious family of Sage Appayya Dikshitar and several other renowned saints and savants, Sri Swami Sivananda had a natural flair for a life devoted to the study and practice of Vedanta. Added to this was an inborn eagerness to serve all and an innate feeling of unity with all mankind.

His passion for service drew him to the medical career; and soon he gravitated to where he thought that his service was most needed. Malaya claimed him. He had earlier been editing a health journal and wrote extensively on health problems. He discovered that people needed right knowledge most of all; dissemination of that knowledge he espoused as his own mission.

It was divine dispensation and the blessing of God upon mankind that the doctor of body and mind renounced his career and took to a life of renunciation to qualify for ministering to the soul of man. He settled down at Rishikesh in 1924, practised intense austerities and shone as a great Yogi, saint, sage and Jivanmukta.

In 1932 Swami Sivananda started the Sivanandashram. In 1936 was born The Divine Life Society. In 1948 the Yoga-Vedanta Forest Academy was organised. Dissemination of spiritual knowledge and training of people in Yoga and Vedanta were their aim and object. In 1950 Swamiji undertook a lightning tour of India and Ceylon. In 1953 Swamiji convened a 'World Parliament of Religions'. Swamiji is the author of over 300 volumes and has disciples all over the world, belonging to all nationalities, religions and creeds. To read Swamiji's works is to drink at the Fountain of Wisdom Supreme. On 14th July, 1963 Swamiji entered Mahasamadhi.

FOREWORD

Start the day with a good, soul-elevating thought. Meditate on the Lord. Repeat His Name. Elevate the mind to the realms divine. Now come out of your meditation room. Look upon the whole world as the Virat-Svarup of the Lord. Feel that the Lord's Divine Energy is flowing through you, serving His own manifestations. Whenever, during the day, this zeal is diminished, recall to the mind the sublime thought-current with which you started the day. Raise the mind to the same level. Thus would you live forever in an exalted state.

A divine perfection of the human being is our aim. That man is capable of self-development and of some approach to an ideal state of perfection which his mind is capable of conceiving, is common to all thinking humanity. But some conceive it as a mere mundane change and others as a total conversion of the human personality. The mundane ideal is something outward, social, political, economic, a rational dealing with our fellow-men and environments, a better and kindlier way of living. It also includes the development of the intelligence, will and reason, a noble ethical, a rich aesthetic, a fine emotional life. Education and the creation of better and favourable social environments is the method adopted for achieving this aim.

The mundane ideal has for its field, the present life and its activities only. Intellectual, emotional, ethical and aesthetic development, political freedom, economic well-being are all good and absolutely necessary for an all-round growth of the individual as well as of the race, but without any definite purpose in life, without any delivering and illuminating aim, they end invariably in frustration. They constitute a constant movement in a circle. To realise the Eternal Truth and to express it through the perfected instruments, the mind and the body, is the principle and whole object of spiritual life and this is the only ideal which can give permanent satisfaction and peace to the thinking mankind.

CONTENTS

Foreword 6

PART I
Spiritual Dynamics in the World of Mind

Chapter 1
Mind: Its Tendencies and Its Transcendence 13

Chapter 2
The Science and Psychology of Thought 19

Chapter 3
Psychoanalysis, Parapsychology and the
    Indian Standpoint. 23

Chapter 4
Spiritual Therapeutics and the Effects of
    Negative Emotions 28

Chapter 5
The Genesis of Human Bondage 35

Chapter 6
False Views and Snares of Delusion 38

PART II
The Psychic World and the Process of Spiritual Evolution

Chapter 7
Concentration, Meditation and Samadhi 47

Chapter 8
Human Nature and the Psychic Pitfalls 53

Chapter 9
Mantra and the Phenomenon of Conscience 57

Chapter 10
The First Steps in Spiritual Evolution 62

Chapter 11
The Spiritual Progressions. 67

PART III
Intuitional Planes and the Structure of the Life Divine

Chapter 12
Intellectual Acrobats and the Spiritual Supermen 70

Chapter 13
Intuitive Experience and Conceptual Knowledge 75

Chapter 14
Foundation of Self-realisation 77

Chapter 15
The Processes of Self-knowledge 83

Chapter 16
The Structure of the Life Divine 87

PART IV
Patterns of Human Greatness

Chapter 17
Cardinal Principles of Greatness 90

Chapter 18
Will-power and the Formation of Personality 97

Chapter 19
Self-development and the Spirit of Selfless Service. . . 101

Chapter 20
The Transcendental Reaches of Blessedness 105

PART V
The Evolutionary Aims and the Techniques of Spiritual Perfection

Chapter 21
The Essentials and the Evolutionary Aims of Life 109

Chapter 22
The Aspirant and the Innate Impetus
Towards the Infinite 114

Chapter 23
Man: His Inheritance and His Destiny 118

Chapter 24
Sadhaka and Some Aspects of Sadhana 122

Chapter 25
Guide and the Spiritual Guidance 128

Chapter 26
The Dynamics of Devotion 132

Chapter 27
Evidences of the Divine Presence 135

Chapter 28
Fate, Fatalism and Free-will 141

Chapter 29
Frowns of Fortune and Spiritual Growth 143

Chapter 30
Continence and the Techniques of Sex-sublimation . . . 147

Chapter 31
Philosophy and Philosophising 152

Chapter 32
Integral Yoga and the Limitations of Science 155

Chapter 33
Vedanta: Its Disciplines and Its Value 165

Chapter 34
Religion: Its Philosophy and Its Purposes 170

APPENDIX
The Enduring Bases for International Ideals 175
Twenty Important Spiritual Instructions 181

DAILY READINGS

PART I
SPIRITUAL DYNAMICS IN THE WORLD OF MIND

Chapter 1
MIND: ITS TENDENCIES AND ITS TRANSCENDENCE

1st January
The Grasshopper Habits of the Mind

Mind is ever restless, never stays on a fixed point for a considerable period. It jumps hither and thither. Mind is ever changing and oscillating. Its wandering habit manifests itself in various ways. The mind in the vast majority of persons has been allowed to run wild and follow its own sweet will, inclinations and desires. The mind of worldly persons is gross: it is not fit for concentration, self-analysis and introspection. Rajasic mind is restless and turbulent: it agitates the body and the senses and makes them subject to foreign influences. An aspirant's mind is calm, collected, sharp and subtle. A well-disciplined mind alone constitutes the powerful process of reaching the highest state of liberation. Spiritual enquiry must be set afloat in the mind.

2nd January
The Housefly Nature of the Mind

The tendency of the mind is always to move downwards. It would rather revel in darkness and multiply and die there, than come and live for a short time in the sunshine, like flowers. Man's mind is something like the housefly. Of course, sometimes, if some sweet-smelling object is kept, it may perch upon it for a moment. But the next moment it would prefer to alight upon a dungheap. Its nature is that. So, perhaps, a nice tune might attract its attention for a while, but the next moment if something is given, to which it is always accustomed, this housefly of the human mind at once goes and sits upon that. It is used to frivolities to mere flippancies. It is used to taunt and give torment to others. When a very delicious dish is put before it, it forgets the spiritual path and alights upon it.

3rd January
The Dog's Tail Human Nature

The workings of Maya through the complex mechanism of the human mind, are so very extremely subtle, so very difficult to overcome, and human nature is fundamentally so Asuric and unregenerate that real spiritual development and progress in Sadhana are indeed very hard to obtain. To achieve success in any measure in the spiritual life is a very difficult and uphill task so much so that truly it is Divine Grace alone that can raise the aspirant from darkness to Light. So vehement, self-assertive and rebellious is the egoistic self of man that it refuses to be changed from its vicious state to a state of virtue, goodness and saintliness. It is a great blunder to think that the mere act of renunciation is a sufficient achievement in spiritual life.

4th January
Mind: Its Machiavelian Movements

One of the vexing paradoxes on the spiritual path is that your mind is both your best friend as also your bitter enemy. Mind becomes a true friend only after being gradually trained to be so. Until then it should be regarded as a troublesome and treacherous enemy inside us. It is extremely diplomatic, cunning and crooked. It is an arch-deceiver. One of the masterstrokes of the mind's artfulness is to make the aspirant feel and smugly imagine that he knows his mind perfectly well and cannot be led away by it and at the same time to delude him totally.

5th January
The Surging Emotions and True Freedom

Physical freedom is no freedom at all. If you are easily carried away by surging emotions and impulses, if you are under the grip of moods, cravings and passions, how can you be really happy? You laugh for five minutes and weep for five hours.

What can wife, sons, friends, fame and power do for you, when you are under the sway of the impulses of your mind? He is a true hero who has controlled his mind. Conquest of the mind is the conquest of the entire world. True victory is over the mind: that is real Freedom. Thorough rigorous discipline and self-imposed restrictions will eventually eradicate all riotous thoughts, wild impulses, cravings and passions. One should become a perfect Yogi.

6th January
The Devilry of the Human Mind

The mind has the knack of making the unwary aspirant confidently think himself its master, while it makes a hopeless fool of him. Its deceptions are subtle. You have heard the saying, "The Devil can quote scriptures for its purpose." Similarly the mind can use a virtue to indulge in a vice. It has an inborn inclination to perversion. It can even take the support of a perfectly good principle seemingly to justify the most unprincipled sort of action. Unless it is scrutinised dispassionately its tricks are never fully discovered.

7th January
The Havoc of Imaginary Fears

Mind works havoc through its power of imagination. Imaginary fears of various sorts, exaggeration, concoction, mental dramatisation, building castles in the air, are all due to this power of imagination. Even a perfectly healthy man has some imaginary disease or other, created by this juggling power of the mind. Imaginary fears involve a tremendous loss of energy. Give up all forms of fear. Constantly meditate upon the Immortal, Indestructible, Fearless Self within you.

8th January
Conquest of the Three Arch-Enemies

Lust, anger and pride are the root of all human ills. They are the enemies of peace and are the parents of all the hosts of evils. Get up in the morning and meditate on the havoc that these three bring about in man's life. If you work yourself up to a feeling that they drain out your vitality—physical and mental—and

DAILY READINGS

your own good, you should eradicate them, then conquest of these three foes will be an easy affair. Victory over these three arch-enemies of man, is the greatest conquest.

9th January
Restless Mind and the Dubious Mastery

You can bore a diamond with a bristle; you can tie an infatuated elephant with a slender silken thread. You can bring the sun down for the play of your child; you can make the flame of fire burn always downwards. But it is difficult to control the mind. For gaining mastery over the mental you have to know what it is, how it works, how it deceives you at every turn and by which methods it can be subdued. As long as the mind restlessly wanders amidst objects, remains fluctuating, excited, agitated, uncontrolled, the true joy of the Self cannot be realised and enjoyed. To control the restless mind and still perfectly all thoughts and cravings is the greatest problem of man. If he has subjugated the mind he is the Emperor of emperors.

10th January
Easy Method for Mind-Control

Do not allow the mind to wander here and there like the strolling street dog. Keep it under your control always. Then alone you can be happy. It must be ever ready to obey you. If the mind says to you "Go eastward", then go westward. If the mind says to you, "Go southward", then march northward. If the mind says to you, "Take a hot cup of tea in winter", then take a cup of icy cold water. Swim like fish against the mental current. You will control the mind quite easily.

11th January
An Exercise for Mental Relaxation

Here is a beautiful daily exercise for mental relaxation. It will pour into you great inspiration and strength. Close the eyes. Think of anything that is pleasant. This will relax the mind in a wonderful manner. Think of the mighty Himalayas, the sacred Ganga, the striking scenery in Kashmir, the Taj Mahal, the Victoria Memorial in Calcutta, a lovely sunset, the vast expanse of ocean or the infinite blue sky. Proceed also this way. Imagine that the whole world and your body are floating like a straw in this vast ocean of the Spirit. Feel that you are in touch with the Supreme Being. Feel that the life of the whole world is pulsating, vibrating and throbbing through you. Feel that the Ocean of Life is gently rocking you on Its vast bosom. Then open your eyes. You will experience immense mental peace.

12th January
Introspective Analysis of the Mind

In introspection the mind itself is the subject of study. A portion of the mind studies the remaining portion of the mind. The higher mind studies the lower mind. Introspection is apperception. Just as you watch the work done by a coolie, a portion of the mind watches the movements of the rest of the mind. By a careful watch, many defects are detected and removed, by suitable Sadhana. Enter a quiet room. Enter into silence daily for about fifteen minutes, morning and evening. Introspect. Watch the mind carefully. You will have to find out through subjective introspection what the mind is exactly doing at a particular time.

13th January
The Techniques of Self-transcendence

Deep introspection alone can reveal a little of the mysterious workings of the mischievous mind. Probe and probe into the mind. Do not be lenient to the mind. The mind will try to compromise with you. Relentlessly hunt out its hidden motives. Subject yourself to keen self-analysis everyday without fail. Oust all sentiments in this process. Become an intelligent, serious and earnest self-C.I.D. Carry on a ceaseless search and a vigorous enquiry inwardly. Pray for the Grace of God who alone can vanquish the mind and enable you to master it. Thus alone, through introspection, analysis, discrimination, vigilance and prayer can you understand the subtle jugglery of this wonderful thing called 'mind' and transcend its deceptions and its tricks.

14th January
Mind-Control by Discrimination

Mind wants repetition of the pleasure once enjoyed. Memory of pleasure arises in the mind; memory induces imagination and thinking. As a consequence attachment arises. Through repetition a habit is formed; habit causes strong Trishna or craving; mind, then, exercises its rule over the poor, helpless, weak-willed worldlings. But as soon as discrimination arises the power of the mind becomes weakened; the mind tries to recede, to retrace its steps to its original home in the heart; the will becomes stronger and stronger when discrimination is awakened. Thanks to Viveka which enables us to get out of this miserable Samsara.

Chapter 2
THE SCIENCE AND PSYCHOLOGY OF THOUGHT

15th January
Studies in Thought

Thought is a vital living force—the most vital, subtle and irresistible force that exists in the universe. Thoughts are living things; they move; they have form, shape, colour, quality, substance, power and weight. You may cease to be, but thoughts can never die. A thought is as much solid as a piece of stone. Thought is the real action; it is a dynamic force. A thought of joy creates sympathetically a thought of joy in others. A noble thought is a potent antidote to counteract an evil thought. Through the instrumentality of thought, you acquire creative power. There are nowadays numerous books on thought-power, thought-dynamics and thought-culture. Study them and possess a comprehensive understanding of thought, its power, workings and usefulness.

16th January
The Marvels of Thought

Every thought that you send out is a vibration which never perishes. It goes on vibrating every particle of the universe and if your thoughts are noble, holy and forcible, they set in vibration in every sympathetic mind. Unconsciously all people who are like you take the thought you have projected and in accordance with the capacity that they have, they send out similar thoughts. The result is that, without your knowledge of the consequences of your own work, you will be setting in motion great forces which will work together and put down the lowly and mean thoughts generated by the selfish and the wicked.

17th January
Spanish Flu and Thought: An Analogy

Thought is very contagious; nay more contagious than the Spanish Flu. A sympathetic thought in you raises a sympathetic thought in others with whom you come in contact. A thought of anger produces similar vibrations in those who surround that angry man. It leaves the brain of one person and enters that of the others who live at long distances and excites them. A cheerful thought produces cheerful thought in others. A smile on your face engenders a smile on those to whom you have directed it. You find yourself filled with joy and intense delight when you see a batch of hilarious children playing mirthfully and dancing in joy.

18th January
Mind: Its Pervasive Power

Thought moves: It actually leaves the brain and hovers about. It enters the brains of others, too. Living in a Himalayan cave, a sage can transmit a powerful thought to any corner of America. And those that try to purify themselves in a cave really purify the world and help it in diverse subtle ways. Nobody can prevent their pure thoughts going and finding their entry into others that are receptive to them. Thought-transference is technically known as telepathy. As mind is Vibhu or all-pervading like ether, thought-transference is possible and is a fact incontroversible.

19th January
Thought: Its Form and Its Name

Suppose your mind is rendered perfectly calm, entirely without thought. Nevertheless, as soon as thought begins to rise, it will immediately take name and form. Every thought has a certain name and a certain form. Thus you find that every idea that man has, or can have, must be connected with a certain word as its counterpart. Form is the grosser and name the finer state of a single manifesting power called thought. But these three are one; wherever there is one, the other two also are there. Wherever name is, there is form and thought.

20th January
The Drawing Power of the Mind

The mind has got a "drawing power": like attracts like, is a great cosmic law. You are continually attracting to yourself, from both seen and unseen side of life-forces, thoughts and conditions most akin to those of your own. Every man has a mental world of his own, his own ideas, his own views, his own sentiments, his own feelings, his own habitual thoughts, his own experiences and his own modes of thinking and into these there constantly come similar ideas, similar views, similar thoughts and experiences.

21st January
Thoughts and Counter-Thoughts

Every thought or emotion or word produces a strong vibration in every cell of the body and leaves a strong impression there. If you know the method of raising an opposite thought, then you can lead a happy, harmonious life of peace and power. Thought of love will at once neutralise a thought of hatred. A thought of courage will immediately serve as a powerful antidote against a thought of fear. Every thought must bring peace and solace to others. It should not bring even the least pain and unhappiness to anyone. Then you are a blessed soul on earth. You can help many, heal thousands, spiritualise and elevate a large number of persons as did Jesus or Buddha.

22nd January
Chemistry of Food and Thought

Mind is directly influenced by the body. Chemical components of different articles vibrate at varying rates. The intake of certain foods sets up discordant vibrations in the physical body. This throws the mind-stuff into a state of oscillation and disequilibrium. Concentration is disturbed. High thinking is rendered difficult, because elevating thoughts imply fine vibrations. The appetites of the physical are to be controlled, the nature of its food strictly regulated.

23rd January
Importance of Positive Thoughts

Thoughts of worry and thoughts of fear are fearful forces within us. They poison the very sources of life and destroy the harmony, the running efficiency, the vitality and vigour. While the opposite thoughts of cheerfulness, joy and courage heal, soothe, instead of irritating, and immensely augment efficiency and multiply the mental powers. Be always cheerful. Smile. Laugh. A good and positive thought is thrice blessed. First, it benefits the thinker by improving his mental body. Secondly, it benefits the person about whom it is entertained. Lastly, it benefits all mankind by improving the general atmosphere.

24th January
The Determining Role of the Last Thought

The last thoughts determine the next birth. The last prominent thought of one's life occupies the mind at the time of death. The predominant idea at the time of death is what in normal life has occupied his attention most. The last thought determines the nature of character of the body to be attained next. As a man thinketh, so shall he become. The last thought of an inveterate drunkard will be that of his peg of liquor. The last thought of a greedy moneylender will be that of his money. The last thought of a mother who is intensely attached to her only son will be that of her son only. The last thought of a man will be the thought of God only if he has disciplined his mind all throughout his life and tried to fix it on God.

Chapter 3
PSYCHOANALYSIS, PARAPSYCHOLOGY AND THE INDIAN STANDPOINT

25th January
Provenances of the Mental Processes

It is an admitted psychological fact that the mental processes by which you obtain knowledge are not merely confined to the field of consciousness but also cover the field of subconsciousness. If you know the technique of speaking to your subconscious mind and the art or science of extracting work from it, all knowledge will be yours. It is a question of practice. All that you have inherited, all that you have brought with you through innumerable crores of births in the past, all that you have seen, heard, enjoyed, tasted, read or known either in this life or in the past lives are hidden in the regions of your inner mind. Why don't you master the technique of concentration and the way of commanding your subconscious and superconscious mind and make the full and free use of all latent powers and knowledge?

26th January
Categories in Indian Psychology

Prana proceeds from Mind. Matter is below Prana. Prana is above Matter but below Mind. Intuition is above reason and is the channel of communication between man and Spirit. Development of the will-power by autosuggestion is the basic principle of Raja-Yoga or Vedanta. Chitta is the subconscious mind. It has two layers: one layer for emotion and the other for passive memory. The instinctive mind is the higher Manas. By Manonasa or annihilation of the mind is meant the destruction or dissolution of the lower nature, desire-mind. Mind occupies an intermediate state between Prakriti and Purusha, Matter and Spirit.

27th January
Theme for a Thesis in Psychology

According to western medical science, light vibrations from outside strike the retina and an inverted image is formed there. These vibrations are carried through optic tract and optic thalamus to the centre of vision in the occipital lobe of the brain in the back part of the head. There, a positive image is formed. Only then does one see the object in front of one. The Vedantic theory of perception is that the mind comes out through the eye and assumes the shape of the object outside. It is only the individual mind that sees objects outside. If you see the same objects through a telescope, they appear different. If you can see with the mind directly, you will have a different vision altogether. Hiranyagarbha or Karya Brahman has a different vision. He sees everything as a vibration within himself, as his own Sankalpa.

28th January
A Psychological Law and Spiritual Development

The nature of the mind is such that it becomes that which it intensely thinks of. Thus, if you think of the vices and defects of another man, your mind will be charged with these vices and defects at least for the time being. He who knows this psychological law will never indulge in censuring others or in finding fault in the conduct of others, will see only the good in others, and will always praise others. This practice enables one to grow in concentration, Yoga and spirituality.

29th January
A Subject for Psychologist's Research

Eyes can only see; ears can only hear; tongue can only taste; skin can only touch; nose can only smell. But the mind can see, hear, taste, touch and smell. All the sense-faculties are blended in the mind. You can see and hear directly through the mind by Yogic practice (clairvoyance and clairaudience). This blows out the Western psychological theory of perception. The five Indriyas are a prolongation of the mind. Mind is a mass of Indriyas. Mind is a consolidated Indriya. Indriya is mind in manifestation. Indriya represents backwaters. The desire in the mind to eat has manifested as tongue, teeth and stomach. If you can control the mind you can control the Indriyas. If you have controlled the Indriyas, you have already controlled the mind.

30th January
ESP and the Subconscious Operations

Even as the sacred Ganga takes its origin in Gangotri, Himalayas, and runs perennially towards Ganga Sagar, the thought-currents take their origin from the bed of Samskaras (impressions) in the inner layers of the mind, wherein are embedded the Vasanas or latent subtle desires, and flow incessantly towards the objects both in waking state and in dreaming state. Practice of telepathy, thought-reading, hypnotism, mesmerism and psychic-healing clearly prove that the mind exists and that a higher mind can influence and subjugate the lower mind. From the automatic writing and the experiences of a hypnotised person, we can clearly infer the existence of the subconscious mind which operates throughout the twenty-four hours. Through spiritual Sadhana change the subconscious mind and be a new being.

31st January
Wireless Telegraphy in Ancient India

Great Yogis like Jnanadev, Bhartrihari and Patanjali used to send and receive messages to and from distant persons through mind-telepathy (mental radio) and thought-transference. Indian telepathy was the first wireless telegraph and telephone service ever known to the World. Thought travels with tremendous velocity through space. Thought has weight, shape, size, form and colour. It is a dynamic force. 'Psychic' transmission of messages by Indian Sages, was a common phenomenon.

1st February
Proofs for Metempsychoses

We have boy-geniuses and child-prodigies. A boy of five becomes an expert in playing piano or violin. Sri Jnanadev wrote his commentary Jnanesvari on the Gita when he was fourteen years old. There had been boy-mathematicians. There was a boy-Bhagavatar who conducted Kathas when he was eight years old. How could you explain this strange phenomenon? This is not a freak of nature. The theory of transmigration only could explain all these things. If a person gets deep grooves in his mind by learning music and mathematics in this birth, he carries these impressions to the next birth and becomes a prodigy in these sciences even when he is a boy.

2nd February
Oriental Wisdom and a Western Theory

The Western psychologists' exposition of dream psychology, though having much to its credit in the shape of research and some valuable information, yet leaves much unexplained. It lacks much that can be supplied only from theories of the East. They can only be explained by thoughtful inferences from the theories of rebirth, the Law of Karma, the operation of external factors like the Akasic records and occult factors like thought-transference and action of astral entities like Pretas of deceased persons. Only a sincere attempt to make a deep study into the working of these factors can form a full and more adequate exposition of the mysterious subject of dream. To the Yogi who has successfully transcended the three states of waking, dream and deep sleep, the knowledge of all these comes perfectly.

3rd February
Psychoanalysis and the Eastern View

That the Western dream theory is sex-ridden, is due to the fact that they start with a wrong notion of what in reality constitutes Man. To them, man is mainly a physical creature endowed with a mind and possessed of a soul. This is just the contrary of the Oriental view that man in reality is a Spirit, expressing himself through the medium of a mind, which has the physical body as its counterpart to function upon the gross external plane. Thus, we see, to the Indian mind, the true Self of man is entirely devoid of sex. It is the body that suffers under the tyranny of a gender. This body is the least part of man as defined by the philosophic mind of the East. Sex is therefore just but one aspect—though a dominant one perhaps—of the individual soul that goes about as Man upon this earthly stage.

Chapter 4

SPIRITUAL THERAPEUTICS AND THE EFFECTS OF NEGATIVE EMOTIONS

4th February
Psychogenic Sources of Diseases

Selfishness, egoism, worry, hatred, contract the blood-vessels, badly damage the nerve-fibres, obstruct the inflow of the vital force or life-current, and lower the vitality and the power of resistance to external forces and influences. Anger generates poison in the blood, in the brain, liver and in the whole system; it produces fever and depression. Hatred causes nervous weakness, uneasiness, restlessness, cough, fever, loss of blood, indigestion, etc. Fear produces low blood pressure and weakness, destroys red blood-cells, makes the face pale, affects the heart, liver and stomach, and produces indigestion, diarrhoea or constipation and impotency. Jealousy will create an inferiority complex, will disable your mind and ruin your health. Jealousy is at the root of the nervous breakdown of millions of people all over the world.

5th February
Psychosomatic Relationship: An Illustrative Instance

A man receives a telegram that his only son died of Pneumonia. At once his face becomes pale; his mind is agitated; he turns nervous; he has no appetite; his red corpuscles are destroyed. If you reflect over this sequence of the whole trouble, you will find that the mind was the first thing to be affected; he received a mental shock and afterwards the entire mechanism of the body reacted to it. This is an instance which should eloquently convince of the influence that the mind exerts on the body. Psychologists are of the opinion that disease is not primarily of the body or of the flesh but of the mind. It is true that disease is caused by the effects on the human system caused by the poisons generated in the blood by anger, revenge, hatred, lust and greed.

6th February
Psycho-physical Parallelism: An Explanation

The body is internally associated with the mind; rather the body is a counterpart of the mind; it is a gross visible form of the subtle, invisible mind. If there is pain in the tooth or in the stomach or in the ear, the mind is at once affected. It ceases to think properly; it is agitated, disturbed and perturbed. If there is depression in the mind, the body also cannot function properly. The pains which afflict the body are called the secondary disease, Vyadhi, while the Vasanas or desires that afflict the mind are termed mental or primary disease, Adhi. Mental health is more important than physical health. If the mind is healthy, the body will necessarily be healthy. If the mind is pure, if your thoughts are pure, you will be free from all diseases. "A sound mind in a sound body."

7th February
The Corroding Effects of Worry and Anger

Worry does great harm to the astral body and mind. Energy is wasted by worry. It causes inflammation and drains the vitality of man. Nothing is gained by the worry-habit. If you are vigilant and keep the mind fully occupied, this worrying-habit will disappear. During intense anger, the whole mind is suffused with black-hue of malice and ill-will, which expresses itself in coils of thunderous blackness, from which fiery arrows of anger dart forth, seeking to injure the one for whom the anger is felt. There is no evil like the emotion of anger: from anger springs delusion, from delusion confusion of memory, from confusion of memory loss of reason! When reason is gone, man is destroyed. In difficult situations, under pain and pleasure, keep the mind rooted in God; you will enjoy undying peace and poise of mind.

8th February
Spiritual Treatment and the Dangerous Effects of Hypnotic Cure

The Great Mahavakya of the Upanishads is "Aham Brahmasmi"—"This Self in me is the Absolute Reality". If that is the Truth, if even the entire universe is only the external manifestation of the potency of a single thought, it must be very simple for an individual to project a thought which has got the potency to destroy the evil effects of a malady and create a curative process by which a disease gets removed. The Yogi knows this trick, and is therefore in a position to cure himself of all diseases and cure others of their diseases. At any rate one can very well think about the rationale behind such mental treatment of physical ills. At the outset, let it be clearly stated that such a treatment is not of the nature of the widely advertised hypnotic cures. In a hypnotic cure, where it succeeds, the hypnotist effects permanent damage to the patient because he gets undue control of the most delicate instrument, the patient's mind. Eventually that mind is rendered incapable of functioning in a normal way even afterwards and, thus, the patient is made a victim. Spiritual treatment on the other hand, is the sending out or the projection of vibrant, forcible, harmonising thought-waves which will take direct control of the patient's mind apparatus, not for the purpose of subordinating it, but for the purpose of charging it with those energies which alone will make that apparatus (the mind) function effectively to do away with the discord-creating tendencies and impulses which are the root-cause of the disease that the patient has been suffering from.

9th February
Methods of Counteracting Psychogenic Factors in Diseases

Very few people realise that evil qualities like hatred, jealousy, anger, touchiness and impatience, are harmful to themselves rather than to those towards whom they are directed. A fit of anger that lasts ten minutes takes away more energy than would the working at the plough for two days without food. Worry, etc., bring on grey hairs scores of years earlier than they are due. Be serene. Look into the good qualities of others, you will hate none. Learn to admire others' achievements, jealousy will disappear. As hatred, doubt, depression generate discordant vibrations in the physical body, counteract them by entertaining cheerfulness, faith, serenity and love which produce good, harmonious, healthy vibrations in the body. By reliance on God, eliminate fear, worry and anxiety.

10th February
Therapeutic Potentialities of Meditation

Meditation is a powerful mental and nervine tonic. The holy vibrations penetrate all the cells of the body and cure the diseases of the body. The powerful, soothing waves that arise during meditation exercise a benign influence on the mind, nerves, organs and cells of the body. The divine energy freely flows like the flow of oil from one vessel to the other, from the feet of all-pervading Lord, to the different parts of the body of the aspirant. Through regular practice of meditation build around yourself a strong fortress of protection against the evil forces of the ignorant world and robe yourself with a magnetic aura.

11th February
The Cell-Theory and the States of Mind

A cell is a mass of protoplasm with nucleus. It is endowed with intelligence. Some cells secrete, while some cells excrete. The cells of the testes secrete semen; the cells of the kidneys excrete urine. Some cells act the part of a soldier. They defend the body from the inroads or attacks of foreign poisonous matter and germs. They digest and throw them out. Some cells carry food materials to the tissues and organs. The cells perform their work without your conscious volition. Their activities are controlled by the sympathetic nervous system. They are in direct communion with the mind in the brain. Every impulse of the mind is conveyed to them. They are greatly influenced by the varying conditions or states of the mind. If there are confusion, depression and other negative emotions in the mind, they are telegraphically transmitted through the nerves to every cell in the body. These soldier cells become panic-stricken. They are weakened. They are not able to perform their functions properly. They become inefficient. Some people are extremely body-conscious, and possess no idea of the Self; they live irregular, indisciplined lives and fill their stomachs with sweets, pastries, and so on. There is no rest for the digestive and the eliminating organs. They suffer from physical weakness and diseases. The atoms, molecules and cells in their bodies produce discordant or unharmonious vibration. They have no hope, confidence, faith, serenity and cheerfulness. They are unhappy. Their life-force is not operating properly. Their vitality is at a low web. Their mind is filled with fear, despair, worry and anxiety. Man's true nature is beyond all states of mind; it is God. By realising the Divine Spirit within himself, man attains perfection, freedom, immortality, bliss eternal.

12th February
Simple Spiritual Prescriptions

The best medicine or panacea for all diseases and for keeping good health is Kirtan, Japa and regular meditation. The Divine waves electrify, rejuvenate, vivify, energise the cells, tissues, nerves. Another cheap but potent drug is to keep oneself always joyful and cheerful. Study Gita, daily one or two chapters with meaning. Keep yourself fully occupied, which is a remedy to keep off thoughts of worldliness. Fill the mind with Sattva and enjoy wonderful health and peace. Obtain an association with the wise, cultivate faith, serenity, truthfulness, courage, mercy, devotion, love, cheerfulness, confidence, divine thought and divine virtues. Allow the mind to run in the spiritual direction, in divine grooves; your mind will be peaceful and generate harmonious vibrations. You will enjoy mental and physical health.

13th February
Meditation, a Preventive, a Germicide, a Tonic, Elixir Divine

There is no better potent antiseptic and germicide in the world than meditation; it kills all sorts of germs, microbes, bacilli, and therefore one may give up food but should never give up one's daily meditation even when one is seriously ailing. What is more, meditation is also a wonderful tonic which tones up the entire system, renovates the cells, removes diseases and checks the development of diseases. Those who meditate save doctor's bills. The fire of meditation annihilates all foulness arising from vice, all miseries and evils emerging from ignorance. Then suddenly comes knowledge or divine wisdom which directly leads to final Emancipation. Meditation is the keeping up of an unceasing flow of God-consciousness.

14th February
Therapeutic Value of Renunciation, Love and Truth

Renunciation removes a host of ailments, such as dyspepsia, rheumatism, diabetes, diseases of liver and intestines and blood pressure; strengthens the heart, brain and nerves. Pure love produces joy, peace of mind, harmonious functioning of the bodily organs, increases the blood qualitatively, and turns the mind towards God. Truth strengthens the heart and mind, brings peace of mind, happiness, inner calmness, spiritual strength and fearlessness.

15th February
Roads to Mental Health

As diseases take their origin in the mind, treat the mind first. The removal of hatred through cosmic love, service, friendship, mercy, sympathy and compassion; removal of greed through disinterested service, generous acts, and charity; the removal of pride through humility—these will help you a great deal in the achievement of good mental health. If bad thoughts are destroyed, many bodily diseases will vanish. God or the Self that resides in the chambers of your heart is the storehouse of health, strength, vigour and vitality. It cannot be affected by germs, microbes, bacilli, cholera, etc. Always think of God; realise the divine Self within you.

Chapter 5

THE GENESIS OF HUMAN BONDAGE

16th February
The Metaphysical Origins of Human Evils

When man identifies himself with his body, his senses, and his mind, he falls into the realm of relativity and is subject to the experience of pleasure and pain, joy and sorrow, gain and loss. It is only through the self-sense or Ahamkara or egoistic consciousness that all the mental cares, dangers and the ever-increasing actions of life arise. There is no greater enemy than Ahamkara or egoism; so long as this is present, it continues to engender in man desires and desires are the wombs of all suffering. In men of egoistic consciousness passion too takes a full hold and makes impossible the birth of divine love.

17th February
The Works of Ignorance

There are two forces in man, one leading him upward and the other leading him downwards to impurity and ignorance. Ignorant persons perform different Karmas with various motives or desires and reap the respective results thereof. But the wise ones do not perform egoistic actions which are never free from taint. The camel eats thorny bushes; blood gushes from its mouth and yet it will never give them up. Even so a worldly man undergoes sufferings and pain and yet he will not abandon his worldliness. Ignorance destroys discrimination and man forgets his duty attaining Self-knowledge or Brahma Jnana.

18th February
Bondage: Its Central Cause

There is no other vessel on this earth to wade the ocean of Samsara than the mastery of the lower instinctive mind. The impure mind is no other than the subtle desires that generate countless births. The tendency to think of sense-objects is indeed the cause of bondage. Liberation means nothing but the destruction of the impure mind. The mind becomes pure when the desires are annihilated. If you have purity of mind, you will remember God; if you always remember God, the knots of the heart, viz., ignorance, desire, and action, will be rent asunder. You will attain Liberation.

19th February
The Hot-Bed of All Aberrations

The erroneous imagination that you are the body, is the root of all evils. Through wrong thinking you identify yourself with the body. Dehaadhyasa arises; you are attached to the body; this is Abhimana. Then Mamata (mineness) arises. You identify yourself with your wife, children, house, and so on. It is identification or attachment that brings about bondage, misery and pain. You never felt miserable when millions of Germans died in the war. Why? Because there was no identification and attachment. But you weep profusely when your son dies, on account of attachment. The word 'my' produces wonderful influence on the mind. Note the difference in effects produced in the mind when you hear the two sentences: 'Horse is dead' and 'My horse is dead'. Empty yourself of egoism. You will be filled with God.

20th February
The Threefold Root of Most Diseases

Most of the diseases take their origin in overeating, sexual excesses and outbursts of anger and hatred. If the mind is kept cool and calm at all times, you will have wonderful health, strength and vitality. Energy is depleted by fits of anger. The cells and tissues are filled with morbid, poisonous materials when one loses one's temper and entertains deep hatred. Many kinds of physical ailments spring up. Various kinds of nervous diseases are attributable to excessive loss of seminal energy and frequent fits of explosive anger or wrath or undesirable emotions. The fire of anger you kindle for your enemy burns yourself. Conquer anger by cultivating serenity. Meditate daily on the ever-tranquil Self or the Eternal which is peaceful, unchanging. You will attain the all-healing virtue of serenity.

21st February
The Genealogy of Miseries

The following is the chain of bondage. From ignorance comes indiscrimination; from indiscrimination, egoism or Abhimana: from egoism, love and hatred; from love and hatred, activities or Karma; from activities, embodiment or taking up of a physical body; from embodiment, miseries. A man whose clothes are caught by fire will immediately run towards water; he will never enquire, how his clothes caught fire. Even so, when you are caught up in this terrible Samsaric wheel of births and deaths with various kinds of miseries, afflictions, pains, you must try your level best to get rid of Ignorance. Develop dispassion, discrimination and enquire "Who, am I?".

Chapter 6
FALSE VIEWS AND SNARES OF DELUSION

22nd February
Instances of Human Delusion

You go to the market in a bright Cadillac, have a peep at the cabaret, visit the Capital, then you step into a cafe with a smart gait, then on to a luxury store to buy a piece of gabardine cloth for a suit—oh yes! you have made none in all these forty days!—and then on your way back to home you see a funeral procession. This creates a sense of renunciation, a vague disgust for mundane things. But in a short time this evaporates. How sad is one's plight when one loses one's property, when one gets an incurable disease, when the bank has failed, when one's son dies. But, even then one does not relinquish one's sinful conduct, one's leech-like tenacity for the 'Venetian show'! Practise eternal vigilance and introspection. Worship and meditate.

23rd February
Deception from Self-Ignorance

The musk-deer does not know that the fragrance of musk is emanating from its own navel. It wanders about here and there to find out the source of this smell. Even so, the deluded ignorant man is not aware that the fountain of bliss is within himself, in his own inner Self. He is running after external perishable objects to get happiness. Each time you search for happiness outside yourself, you wander away from its real source. Turn inwards. The highest happiness can be had through Self-realisation. Pleasure depends on nerves, mind and objects; happiness is independent and self-existent; it is in yourself.

24th February
The Phantom of Reputation

Even noble minds run after the shadowy toys of name and fame. Name and fame are illusory, mere vibrations in the air. Nobody can earn an everlasting name in this Mayayic plane. Does anybody remember Sri Vyasa, Vasishtha, Vikramaditya, Yajnavalkya, Vamadev, Jada-Bharata, now, except remembering one or two political leaders? A few years hence, the names of these political potentates will disappear. Treat earthly reputation as paltry. Consecrate your life to selfless service, without a view to cut a fine figure. Contact the everlasting Reality.

25th February
The Treacherous Frankenstin's Monster

Man is plagued on by the sense-pleasures he creates. Every type of sense-enjoyment has hidden beneath its velvety cover, a ferocious tigress! Lust eats away man's intelligence; wealth brings with it restlessness. Family means worry! Even if fortune smiles on him, the inevitable Old Age creeps in. The pleasure-centres which sustained him during his youth and manhood, haunt him now. Enjoyment cannot bring satisfaction of desire. On the contrary, it aggravates and intensifies desires and makes the mind more restless through sense-hankering, just as the pouring of oil increases the fire. The fewer the wants, the greater the happiness.

26th February
Illusion Originating from Excessive Extroversion
The senses have been created with a natural tendency to flow out towards the objective universe. The externalisation dissipates the rays of the mind, weakens the intellect and blinds the eye of intuitive perception: Unity is falsely represented as diversity: the untrue appears to be true: pain appears to be pleasure: and shadow holds out greater charms than the Substance Itself. This is the path of "Preyas" (the pleasant) which the dull-witted ignorant man pursues.

27th February
The Great Illusion
A doctor thinks that the Advocate is very happy. The Advocate thinks that a businessman is more happy. The Judge thinks that the Professor is more happy. This is an illusion. This is a trick of the mind. Verily, no one is really happy in this world. Real happiness can only be had in one's own Atman. Therefore attain Self-realisation and be happy.

28th February
The Two Types of Fools
In this world there are two types of fools: (i) those who imagine that their body is the pure Atman and that there is nothing beyond the senses, and (ii) those who think that they are Brahma-Jnanis after studying Brahma-Sutras, Upanishads or Panchadasi. If you want to be wise, remember God; sing His Name; feel His Presence. Speak truth. Learn to discriminate. Learn how to lead a divine life while remaining in the world. Serve society with Atma-bhava, with the feeling that all persons are manifestations of God. You will soon regain your Godhead.

29th February
The Web of Man

The spider pours out of its mouth long threads and weaves them into cobwebs and gets itself entangled in the net of its own making. Even so, man makes a net of his own ideas, conceptions and abstractions and gets entangled in it. The wise man should therefore abandon all worldly thoughts, sophisticated ideas and know his own essential nature.

1st March
Suspicion and Its Beclouding Power

Suspicion is conjecture with imperfect or with little or no evidences to support it, that something, especially something wrong, exists or is about to happen. It is unreasonable imagination or apprehension. Ignorance is the mother of suspicion. Suspicion clouds the mind, creates rupture among friends. It is mistrust and doubt. Suspicion is the mark of a mean spirit and a base soul. It is a defect not in the heart, but in the brain.

Never suspect anyone. Make others truly happy as you strive to make yourself happy. Speak a helpful word. Give a cheering smile. Do a kind act. Serve a little. Render smooth a rough place in another's path. You will feel great joy.

2nd March
Appearances Are Deceptive

Let not appearances deceive you. There goes the devotee, chanting the sacred Name of Narayana. He sings in ecstasy and dances in rapture for an hour or two. He is vehement in asserting that all indeed is Narayana. Here is a great monist who would not stop repeating: 'I am God', 'I am God', 'I am God'. Profound is his learning, and mighty his swordsmanship in argument. Tarry a while, friend. Watch them under three conditions. When desperately hungry, when bitterly provoked and insulted, and when another man is pathetically distressed. Now if they fulfil their former assertions, all hail to them, veritable gods on earth are they; if they do not, keep yourself aloof from them lest you should be infected.

3rd March
True Freedom and the Inextricable Snares of Ignorance

Hindu and Buddhist thinkers, with a singular unanimity declare that Avidya (ignorance) is the source of our anguish and all our trouble. Man's nature of oneness with the living universe is lost. He develops an egocentric view of life and puts his individual preference above social welfare, He develops an acquisitive instinct and looks upon every other being as his potential enemy. He clings to nature, to his neighbours, in short, to everything, which is evanescent. He becomes a divided being, tormented by doubt, fear, suffering. There is a split in his oneness. The world lives in incessant fear. Religion is the conquest of fear, an antidote to failure and death. We cannot dispel our doubts by drugging ourselves with illusions. True freedom from fear is gained by Wisdom.

4th March
Inseparable Pairs of Opposites

Pleasure and pain, gain and loss, life and death, good and evil are the obverse and reverse sides of the same coin. Evil cannot exist without good; life, without death. They are relative terms. Ignorant people want everlasting happiness in this world: this is simply puerile. Pleasure and pain, life and death are inseparably linked together. If you do not want pain and death, give up sensual pleasures and existence in physical limitations.

5th March
Fictitious Distinctions

Distinctions of caste, creed, colour have absolutely no place in matters of faith. A true devotee recognises the equality of all men. When the inner eye of wisdom is opened, when the aspirant beholds oneness everywhere, when he feels the presence of the Lord in every atom of the universe, where are the distinctions of caste, creed, colour? It is the fleshy, dirty eye of a worldly-minded man, that perceives these illusory distinctions. See life as a whole. The Lord breathes in all life. The world is one home. All are members of one human family. Cultivate cosmic love. Include all. Recognise the worth of others. Destroy all barriers that separate man from man.

6th March
Troupe of Sorrows Attendant Upon Each Sensuous Enjoyment

Sensual enjoyment is attended with various defects. It is attended with various sorts of sins, pains, weaknesses, attachments, slave mentality, weak will, severe exertion and struggle, bad habits, cravings, aggravation of desires and mental restlessness. Therefore shun all sorts of sensual enjoyments. Look out for an unchangeable, infinite and supreme happiness which must come from a Being in whom there is no change.

7th March
Impacts that Constitute Evil Company

Reading of newspapers and sensational novels kindles worldly Samskaras, causes crude movements in one's being, engenders sensational excitement in the mind, makes the mind outgoing, produces an impression that the world is a solid reality and makes one forget the Truth that lies underneath these names and forms. Bad surroundings, obscene pictures, obscene songs, plays that deal with love, cinemas, theatres, the sight of pairing of animals, words which give rise to bad ideas in the mind, in short, anything that causes evil thoughts and sentiments constitutes evil company and therefore should be avoided and shunned by all aspirants. The effects of evil company and association with undesirable persons and things, are highly disastrous to one's upward progress and spiritual growth.

8th March
The Effects of Evil Company

Just as a nursery is to be well-fenced in the beginning, as a measure in the protection of it against cows, and other animals, so also a neophyte should shield himself against all foreign evil influences. Otherwise ruination will result. The company of those who speak lies, commit adultery, cheat, indulge in double- dealing, are greedy, love idle talks and backbiting, have no faith in God and in the scriptures, should be strictly avoided. The effects of evil company are highly disastrous. By contact with such a company, the mind gets filled with bad ideas. Undesirable persons easily shake your faith and belief. Have full faith in your spiritual teacher and continue your spiritual practice with zeal and enthusiasm.

9th March
Fifteen Evils of Company

There are fifteen doshas or evil effects that arise from company. An aspirant who is ardently pursuing his spiritual Sadhana, should, therefore, preferably remain alone during the period of his practice. The doshas are: (1) Misunderstanding; (2) Ill-feeling; (3) Displeasure; (4) Raga-dvesha, likes and dislikes; (5) Jealousy; (6) Vampirism; (7) Attachment; (8) Mental sharing of pain of another man; (9) Criticisms of others; (10) Worldly topics; (11) Habit of talking; (12) Slavish mentality and weak will; (13) Bahirmukha vritti (outgoing tendency of the mind); (14) Idea and Samskara of duality; (15) Contempt.

10th March
Exhibitions of Talent Hinder Higher Aspirations

An exhibition of one's abilities brings physical comforts through objective contact, invigorates the ego and strengthens the sense of individuality. These comforts act as powerful hindrance for the higher aspirations of the soul. Therefore one should use the wisdom he possesses for the purpose of inner meditation and spiritual attachment and never for external pursuits in the world. Fie upon that wisdom which is used for bringing pleasures to the ego.

11th March
The Torment of Tantalus

Craving is the "will-to-live" of Schopenhauer, "tanha" of Lord Buddha, "Abhinivesa" of Patanjali Maharshi. Craving is Trishna; it is intense inner sense-hankering; it includes thought and desires. Craving is the germ of personality. It is the flame of the life of appetites. It is the cause for pain, sorrow, unhappiness and births and deaths. It builds the false ego. It strengthens and fattens the ego. There is no end to craving in the life of a worldly man; for this reason, he is, despite his wealth and comforts, ever restless. Quench this flame through dispassion, renunciation and meditation and attain the bliss of the Eternal.

Live for God. Boldly face all the difficulties and tribulations of this petty, earthly life. Be a man. With courage, struggle for the Great Attainment. Climbing a mountain, crossing a channel, bombing a city, or blasting a fort—these are not the true acts of heroism. Controlling your mind and senses, and overcoming anger, passion and egoism by attaining self-mastery—these constitute the real heroism in man. How long will you be a slave of passion and the senses? Assert your real divine nature, and your mastery over your lower nature and lower self. This is your most important duty.

PART II

THE PSYCHIC WORLD AND THE PROCESS OF SPIRITUAL EVOLUTION

Chapter 7

CONCENTRATION, MEDITATION AND SAMADHI

12th March

The Miraculous Powers of Mind

There was a blind saint in Maharashtra, who could take any book and read well without any hesitation. This is no marvel because he developed the inner psychic sight and could directly see with the mind itself—clairvoyance—without the aid of the physical eye. Every man can do this by practice of Sadhana. The mind can see, hear, taste, smell and feel by itself without the help of the Indriyas. In the mind, all the Indriyas are blended. Mind has immense powers. It derives these powers from the inner Spiritual Being. If you can check the dissipation of its energies by worry, evil thoughts, cares, anxieties and lack of Brahmacharya, and control the immense amount of power which it possesses, through concentration, sublime divine thoughts, you will acquire Siddhis or miraculous powers and the capacity to do supernatural actions.

13th March

Aids to Concentration

A man whose mind is filled with passion and all sorts of fantastic desires can hardly concentrate on any object even for a second. Celibacy, Pranayama, reduction of wants and activities, renunciation of sensual objects, solitude, silence, discipline of the senses, annihilation of lust, greed, anger, non-mixing with undesirable persons, giving up of newspaper reading and visiting exciting cinemas—all these increase the powers of concentration. Concentration is possible and most successful only when you are free from all distractions. Concentrate on anything that appeals to you as good or anything which the mind likes best. Regularity in the practice is of paramount importance.

14th March
Twenty Techniques that Heighten Power of Concentration

The observance of celibacy, the practice of Pranayama, the curtailment of wants and desires, the reduction of worldly activities, resort to silence, remaining in seclusion in a room for one or two hours daily, the raising of prayers, the exercise of discrimination, or Vichara, discipline of the senses, control of anger, non-mixing with undesirable persons, annihilation of greed and selfishness, control over the bodily posture through Yoga Asanas, freedom from disturbing sensations or thoughts of work on hand, increase in the number of sitting in daily meditation, repetition of inspiring scriptural hymns, expression of mercy and love for all, development of the powers of attention, reflection on the miraculous benefits of obtaining full concentration, a burning aspiration to realise the Divine Being within the span of present life, the presence of past spiritual tendencies,—are the twenty techniques or methods for increasing and heightening the powers of concentration. One who has developed great powers of concentration obtains intuition, evolves rapidly, acquires immense inner spiritual strength, and gains unalloyed spiritual felicity and communion with God.

15th March
Benefits of Concentration

Through concentration one gets penetrative insight—subtle esoteric meanings will flash out in the field of mental consciousness. One will understand the inner depths of philosophical significance when one reads Gita or Upanishads with concentration. Those who practise concentration possess a very good health and very cheerful mental vision and spiritually evolve quickly. Concentration purifies and calms the surging emotions, strengthens the current of thought and clarifies the ideas. Nothing is impossible for one who practises regular concentration.

16th March
Inspirational Value of Meditation

The practice of meditation itself is a potent clarifier of the memory and an inspirer of discriminative thought. During meditation, when the mind is rendered more Sattvic and pure and calm, you will feel highly inspired and your mind will be composing fine poems and solving intricate problems of life. But then, you should stamp out these Sattvic Vrittis, transcend this level of inspiration, go beyond the artistic expression. For such activities too go to dissipate the inner spiritual energy which should be conserved for soaring higher and higher in the realms of the Divine Experience.

17th March
Initial Results of Regular Meditation

Regular meditation opens the avenues of intuitional knowledge, makes the mind calm and steady, awakens an ecstatic feeling and brings the Yogic student in contact with the source of the Supreme Purusha. If there are doubts, they are all cleared by themselves when you march on the Path of Dhyana Yoga steadily. You will yourself feel the way to place your footstep on the next rung of the spiritual ladder. A mysterious inner voice will guide you. Hear this attentively.

18th March
The Man of Meditation

The Mahatma who meditates in a solitary cave in the Himalayas helps the world more through his spiritual vibrations than the Sadhu who preaches on the platform. Just as sound vibrations travel in the ethereal space, so also the spiritual vibrations of meditator travel a long distance and bring peace and strength to thousands. When the meditator becomes mindless, he pervades and permeates the whole world. Ignorant people bring a false charge that the Sadhus, who meditate in caves are selfish. Just as the sweet fragrance of jasmine pervades the air, so also his spiritual aura becomes infiltrated into the minds of others. People draw from him, joy, peace, and strength, and experience an elevation of mind by mere contact with him.

19th March
The Influence of a Developed Mind

Mark the influence of a highly developed mind over a less developed mind! It is not possible to describe what it is like to be in the presence of a Master or a developed adept. To sit in his presence, though he hardly speaks a word, is to feel a thrilling sensation so much as to feel new inspirations touching one mentally. Mind has got aura (mental aura or psychic aura). Aura is Tejas, brilliance or halo that emanates from the mind. The aura of those who have developed their minds is extremely effulgent. It can travel long distance and affect in a beneficial manner a large number of persons who come under its influence. The spiritual aura is more powerful than either the psychic or Pranic aura. He who has purified his mind becomes a centre of force. All the lesser minds are unconsciously drawn towards him.

20th March
The Diversity of Approach

Samadhi means super-consciousness. Samadhi is loss of one's personality in the Divine. It is deliverance from delusion of personality. A Bhakta gets Bhava Samadhi through lofty feelings; a Raja Yogi gets Nirodha Samadhi through restraint of thought-waves; a Jnani gets Bhada Samadhi through negation of names and forms. Deep meditation leads to Samadhi or oneness with God. The mind is filled with God. Just as a toy made of salt melts in Brahman in Nirvikalpa Samadhi. A sudden stroke of mystic illumination puts an end to all the empirical existence altogether.

21st March
Samadhi and Certain Similar Mental States

For a short time, sometimes the mind finds itself in quiescence. In this state of mind there is neither Raga nor Dvesha; this silent mental state is called Tushnim Avastha. It occurs in waking state, the Jagrat Avastha. The aspirant mistakes this neutral state of mind, for Samadhi. This is an obstacle on the path of God-realisation, and should, therefore, be overcome by careful introspection and vigorous meditation. Through experience and acute acumen, a Sadhaka can find out exactly the nature of the various states of mind. He should adopt effective methods to control them.

22nd March
Samadhi: An Issue of Long-continued Diligency of Herculean Effort

Samadhi is difficult of attainment. Do not mistake brooding, building castles in the air and half-sleepy state for Samadhi. Great is the glory of a man of Samadhi; he can move the whole world. Mere juvenile enthusiasm, emotional bubbling, will not bring the desired results. Aspire to purify yourself first. Become an embodiment of love, mercy and goodness. One has to apply oneself to Sadhana, diligently, day and night. Like the man who anxiously seeks a means of escape from the midst of a burning house, the aspirant should have a burning desire to free himself from the fire of Samsara. Only then will he be able to enter into deep meditation and Samadhi.

23rd March
Ineffable Nature of the Highest Spiritual Experience

Spiritual experiences cannot be described in words. Language is imperfect. They are to be felt and realised by the aspirants. Experiences vary. A devotee, a Yogi and a sage have different spiritual experiences in the beginning. Ultimately, the highest experience is one and invariable. The highest experience is that in which you become identical with the Absolute.

There is neither darkness nor void in this experience. It is all-light. You become a Sarvavid or all-knower. You know the mystery of creation. You get immortality, higher knowledge, and eternal bliss.

In meditation, new grooves are formed in the brain, and the mind moves upwards in the new spiritual grooves. When the mind becomes steady in meditation, the eyeballs also become steady. A Yogi whose mind is calm will have a steady eye.

There will be no winking at all. The eyes will be lustrous, red or pure white.

When you enter into very deep, silent meditation, the breath will not come out of the nostrils. There may be occasional, slow movement of the lungs and the abdomen.

In profound and continued meditation, thinking ceases. There is only one idea of "I am the Infinite", "Aham Brahmasmi". When this idea also is given up, Nirvikalpa Samadhi ensues. Just as salt melts in water, the Sattvic mind melts in the Brahman, its Substratum.

Chapter 8

HUMAN NATURE AND THE PSYCHIC PITFALLS

24th March
Season for the Ascent of the Animal in Man

The whole mango tree with branches, leaves and fruits is contained in a subtle form in the seed. It takes time for manifestation. Even so the Vasana of lust lurks in the mind when you are a boy, manifests at eighteen, fills the whole body at twenty-five. Mind havocs from twenty-five to forty-five, and then it gradually declines. Various forms of wrong-doing and mischief are done by human beings between 25 and 45. This is the most critical period of life. There is no particular difference between a boy and a girl in their characteristics when they are too young. After attaining puberty they exhibit their characteristic qualities.

25th March
Perilous Pitfalls on the Path—I

Right from the very beginning of one's spiritual life, one must understand clearly that in true 'humanity'—sincere desire to root out gradually pride, egoism and jealousy, earnest and unceasing introspection to find out one's own defects and improve oneself—lies one's hope of progress. Without this basis, any form of Sadhana becomes a delusion and a waste. It makes the aspirant puffed up, more proud and egoistic. When this happens, all good advice and instructions fall flat upon him. Higher influences cease to have any effect as the aspirant becomes deliberately and obstinately non-receptive to them. Eternal vigilance should be exercised if he is to avoid falling into this dangerous state. Spiritual life is not a light matter.

26th March
Perilous Pitfalls on the Path—II

Sinning and evil has become so much a habit with man that he never feels that he is committing them even though day and night he is doing so constantly. And the greatest harm is done by the fact that even while in this unregenerate state, the aspirant becomes deluded by Maya into thinking that he has already progressed considerably in spirituality. He deceives himself with the thought that as far as he is concerned he is pretty advanced in Sadhana. He thinks that he has acquired that Nirlipta (unattached) attitude where he can commit any form of act and yet remain unaffected by it.

Under this grave delusion he allows himself to be unrestrained and runs wild, intolerant of criticism, resentful of the least opposition, utterly disregardful of others' feelings and absolutely unamenable to advice and correction. All sense of discrimination, sane judgment and introspection vanish from him. Even the common courtesy and culture possessed by an ordinary worldly man take leave of the aspirant on account of his presumption of spiritual advancement and growth in wisdom. He becomes disposed to attack even venerable and elderly persons and spiritually superior souls. Fully realise the importance of becoming a changed man ethically and morally, before you can claim to be a Sadhaka. The aspirant should carefully avoid the dangers of self-deception by constant vigilance and introspection. When his nature is changed, purified and prepared, the Divine Grace will spontaneously flood his Heart and enlighten him.

27th March
Perilous Pitfalls on the Path—III

The wandering habit of the mind is one of the big hurdles on the path. It manifests itself in various ways. A householder's mind wanders to the cinema, theatre, circus, etc. A Sadhu's or monk's mind wanders to Varanasi, Brindavan, and other places of pilgrimage. Many Sadhus do not stick to one place during Sadhana. The wandering habit of the mind must be controlled by rendering it chaste and constant by Vichara. The mind must be trained to stick to one place for five years during your meditative life, to one method of Sadhana, to one path of Yoga, to one spiritual objective, and to one guide.

28th March
Spiritual Realisation and Psychic Pitfalls

Various psychic Siddhis and other powers come to the Yogi who has controlled his senses, Prana and mind. But all these are hindrances to spiritual realisation. They are stumbling blocks; they allure the Yogic students. Temptations of the astral, mental and Gandharva worlds are more powerful than the earthly temptations. Unwary students are overwhelmed by them. One is bound to get some psychic powers, as a result of regular practice of meditation and concentration; but to use these powers for base and selfish purposes, for gaining some material end, will be disastrous.

29th March
Supernormal Powers and Spiritual Experience

During the course of his Sadhana, the aspirant acquires some experiences, sees wonderful vision of Rishis, Mahatmas, astral entities of various description, hears various melodious sounds, smells Divya Gandha, gets the powers of thought-reading, foretelling, etc. Now, the aspirant foolishly imagines that he has reached the highest goal and stops his further Sadhana. He slips into false Tushti or false contentment. This is a serious mistake. These visions, these experiences and these powers are not in themselves the culminating point in the Sadhana. Abandon the idea of these experiences and powers. The final experience, intuitional and direct, of the Supreme alone is the true one.

30th March
Psychic Powers and Real Yoga

Do not think too much of psychic Siddhis. Clairvoyance and clairaudience are not worth having when far greater illumination and peace are possible without the Siddhis. Desire for powers will act like puffs of air which may blow out the lamps of Yoga that is being carefully tended. Any selfish desire for Siddhis will blow out the little spiritual light that the Yogi has kindled after so much struggle and will hurl the student down into the deep abyss of ignorance. He will not be able to rise up again to the original height which he has ascended on the hill of Yoga.

Chapter 9
MANTRA AND THE PHENOMENON OF CONSCIENCE

31st March
The First-Fruits of Prayer

Prayer generates good spiritual currents and produces a rare tranquillity of the mind; it elevates the whole emotional nature and is accompanied by the growth of inward grace, inner strength, and a sense of atonement with the Supreme Being. The intensive purified feelings raised in acts of prayer, bring about the most beneficial inner change in the heart; the receptive attitude of the silenced praying mind puts the soul of man in tune with the Infinite, links it with the cosmic powerhouse of inexhaustible energy and surcharges it with strength, grace, energy, light. When prayers are raised on foundations of absolute devotion, purity of motive, detachment from all worldly concerns, and unyielding faith in the Divine, they lead the inner being of man into highest spiritual Experience.

1st April
Psychological Consideration of Prayer

Psychologically, it should be remembered that prayer is not merely uttering of words but an intense and sincere feeling of and a longing for contact with a Power which is all-pervading, which includes everything within itself, and which is the most real of all beings. The nature of thinking and feeling is such that it is not possible to think of or feel anything without transforming the psychological organ into the mode of the object which is thought or felt. And because, in the case of prayer, the object is infinite Power itself, the mind takes such a powerful mode, that the devotee gets endowed with superhuman powers in addition to his achieving the purpose for which the prayer is offered.

2nd April
Mantra: Its Force and Its Functions

As a result of repetition, through the force of Samskaras, the Mantra gathers creative momentum. A Mantra is a mass of radiant energy or Tejas. It transforms the mental substance by producing a particular thought movement. The rhythmical vibrations produced by its utterance regulate the unsteady vibrations of the five sheaths or the Pancha-koshas. It checks the natural tendencies of the mind to run after sensuous objects. It helps the Sadhana Sakti and reinforces it when it becomes imperfect and meets with obstacles. Sadhana-Sakti is strengthened by Mantra-Sakti and when the sleeping consciousness in a Mantra or the Mantra Chaitanya is awakened, the Mantra awakens in the Sadhaka superhuman powers or Siddhis.

3rd April
Rationale of the Mantra-Repetition

Mantra is Daivi Sakti, Divine Power, manifesting in a sound-body. Constant repetition of the Mantra with faith, devotion and purity augments the Sakti of the aspirant, purifies and awakens the Mantra Chaitanya latent in the Mantra and bestows on the Sadhaka Mantra Siddhi, illumination, freedom, peace and immortality. By constant repetition of the Mantra the Sadhaka imbibes the virtues and powers of the Deity that presides over the Mantra. Repetition of Surya Mantra bestows health, vigour, vitality, 'brilliance,' removes bodily and eye diseases, and wards off all danger and harm. The repetition of a Mantra has a mysterious power of bringing about the manifestation of the Divinity, just as the splitting of an atom manifests the tremendous forces latent in it.

4th April
Particular Mantras for Particular Benefit

The repetition of the Subrahmanya Mantra 'Om Saravanabhavaaya Namah' will give you success in any undertaking and make you glorious. It will drive off the evil influences and evil spirits. Repetition of Sri Hanuman Mantra 'Om Hanumanthaaya Namah', will bestow victory and strength. Repetition of Panchadasakshara and Sodasakshara (Sri Vidya) will give you wealth, power, freedom, etc. The Maha Mrityunjaya Mantra will save you from accidents, incurable diseases, and calamities, and bestow on you long life and immortality. It is a Moksha-mantra, too. Those who do Japa of this Mantra daily will enjoy good health and long life, and attain Moksha or Liberation in the end.

5th April
Miraculous Uses of the Mantras

Chanting of Mantras generates potent spiritual waves of divine vibrations. They penetrate the physical and astral bodies of the patients and remove the root causes of sufferings. They fill the cells with pure Sattva or divine energy. They destroy the microbes and vivify the cells and tissues; they are the best, most potent antiseptics and germicides. They are more potent than ultra-violet rays or Roentgen rays.

6th April
The Rational Character of Miracles

The divine touch of sages healing incurable diseases and at times even bestowing back life to the dead are actually facts in the spiritual realm. These miracles baffle reason, no doubt; but, more often than not the miracle implies not merely the nullifying of known law but rather the evoking and bringing into play of a higher law of which the uninformed observer is quite unaware. Hence the latter's wonder and astonishment at the occurrence. When the cause is hidden from your ken and in the absence of the connecting sequence the effect alone is beheld, you feel it as something supernatural.

7th April
The Counsel of the Conscience

Conscience is a sensitive balance to weigh actions; it is a guiding voice from within. When you do a wrong action, the conscience pricks you. You experience pinpricks. It says to you in a clear, small, shrill voice: "Do not do this wrong action my friend. It will bring misery to you." A conscientious man at once ceases to act wrongly and further and becomes wise. Cowardice asks: "Is it safe?". Avarice asks: "Is there any gain in it?" Vanity asks: "Can I become famous?" Lust asks: "Is there pleasure?" But Conscience asks: "Is it right?". Conscience prompts you to choose the right instead of the wrong, and tells you that you ought to do the right.

8th April
The Evolution of Conscience

According to the state of his knowledge man's conscience is built up and changes from time to time with the correction of his views, in the light of further knowledge gained subsequently. The conscience of a child or a savage is entirely different from the conscience of a fully grown civilised man and even amongst civilised men knowledge varies so much that their consciences direct different lines of conduct. The conscience of a Sattvic man is very clean and very pure. The conscience of Ramji will not allow him to do one thing, but the conscience of Chatterji may allow him to do that very thing. Therefore, you cannot rely on conscience entirely, until you have cleared your mind and feeling from personal prejudice and predilections. Never mistake the lower mind's promptings for the voice of the soul.

9th April
Reversal in the Sensitivity of Conscience

If an honest man begins to take bribes for the first time, he shudders; for, his conscience quivers and trembles; he feels a lot of uneasiness. But if he repeats it again several times, his conscience becomes blunt. He ceases to feel any uneasiness. If a chaste man visits for the first time, a house of ill-fame, his conscience pricks and makes him shudder. But, if he visits that house frequently, his conscience loses its sensitiveness and becomes blunt. He will not feel anything. Therefore, understanding the fact that the inner mechanism of conscience is very subtle, always try to keep it sensitive, by doing virtuous deeds only.

10th April
Discernment of the Right Action

When something is done, if there ensues as your personal experience joy, exhilaration or satisfaction, understand that you are doing right action; but if you experience fear, shame, doubt or pricking of conscience, know that you are doing a wrong action. A constant awareness of the Divine, eliminates all possible tendencies to wrong action: this will empower your mind with a strongly marked moral judgment which will discern easily and pronounce if a particular action be right or wrong, good or bad. Whenever you perform an action, if you experience an elevation of mind, a sense of ease and brightness, know that action to be right.

Do not do any act which brings no good to others or which will make you repent later on or ashamed. Do such acts which are praiseworthy and which bring good to you and to others. This is a brief description of right conduct. Moral precepts have been made to free one another from all injuries.

It is the motive that counts in the performance of an action. Right and wrong are to be determined, not by the objective consequences, but by the nature of the subjective intention of the agent. God looks to the motive of the doer.

Chapter 10

THE FIRST STEPS IN SPIRITUAL EVOLUTION

11th April
Equipment Preparatory to the Spiritual Venture

A thorough study of the natural laws and truths of life is absolutely necessary before venturing into the spiritual path. Without the necessary equipments such as your conviction about the unreality of earthly life, and without burning dispassion and self-restraint, by taking to the spiritual path you are liable to be lost in the dark dungeon of despair and frustration. There is no use in keeping your legs in two boats.

Exhibit undaunted spirit and manliness. Make a strong resolve: "I will die or realise."

12th April
Personal Demand and Bewildering Number of Doctrines

In a bazaar you will see many things for which you have no use. But then why do you blame the shop-keeper for it. Even so the different kinds of Yoga, the different kinds of scriptures: Puranas, Agamas, Nigamas, Philosophies, etc., have their own utility. To suit all sorts of men, all sorts of systems are useful and necessary. Why should you count pebbles on the river bed? Your business is to drink water if you are thirsty.

13th April
Necessaries of Spiritual Development

Unfavourable conditions, certain amount of mental restlessness, sense of frustration, a little of unhappiness in life can never be avoided; for, they are evolutionary necessity with every human being, they are the conditions of upward ascent and spiritual growth. Every spiritual aspirant must possess infinite power of endurance and great patience and make persistent strenuous efforts at achieving Divine Illumination, Peace, Joy and Glory. Let the Sadhana be regular, continuous, unbroken, and earnest. If quick God-realisation is your aim, both regularity and continuity in Sadhana and meditation are required. Never stop Sadhana until you are fully established in God-consciousness.

14th April
First Things First

Any number of zeroes have no intrinsic value unless number 1 (one) is added before them. Even so the wealth of the three worlds is nothing if you do not try to acquire spiritual wealth, if you do not strive for Self-realisation. Therefore live in the soul or the Self within. Add the Divine to the Life here. Seek first the Lord within: He is the fountain-source of Divine Riches, Power and Beauty.

DAILY READINGS

15th April
Divine Will and the Only Human Duty
Even a dry leaf cannot be wafted by the strongest gale without His Will, and as we are all His beloved children, His will cannot but work out to our good. He being the indweller knows what is good for us; not we. To rejoice at what He gives us, resting where He places us, taking all that comes as His blessing and repeating His Name, glorifying Him in all our actions, words and thoughts—that alone is our duty.

16th April
The Pattern of Saintliness
The beginning of saintliness is killing of egoism. The end of saintliness is Eternal life. The key to saintliness is Brahmacharya. The light of saintliness is universal love. The garb of saintliness is virtue. The mark of saintliness is equal vision. The road to saintliness is regular meditation. The foundation of saintliness is Yama-Niyama. A saint lives in God: he is God-intoxicated.

17th April
Incomparable Friends and Formidable Foes
There is no eye like intuition, no blindness like ignorance, no evil like lust, no enemy like anger. There is no friend like Atman, no virtue like Satyam, no shelter like the lotus feet of the Lord, no wealth like the spiritual wealth. Therefore develop the eye of intuition, eradicate ignorance and lust, kill this enemy anger, make friendship with Atman and attain the Supreme Wealth of God-realisation.

There is no greater obstacle to divine life and meditation than the craving on carnal pleasures. Kill this craving through enquiry, dispassion and meditation. Flesh is your invulnerable foe. Live in the Spirit or Atman and annihilate this formidable foe. March forward, O brave soldier!

18th April
Pursuit of the Eternal Values
There is no light like that of knowledge of the Self or Brahman. There is no treasure like that of contentment. There is no virtue

like that of truthfulness. There is no bliss like that of the soul. There is no friend like Atman. Therefore know your own Self. Develop contentment. Speak the truth. Drink the bliss of the soul.

19th April
Dependence on the Divine

Be frank and confess all your troubles before Him. Speak to Him like a child. Even before you express, the Lord understands your difficulties. He is the life of your life, Soul of your soul. Depend upon Him alone. All other help will fail, but this divine company will never fail. Ever repeat His Name. He will take care of you.

Rely on God alone. Do not depend on money, friends, or anyone. When the friends are put to test, they will desert you. Lord Buddha never relied even on his disciples. When he was seriously ailing, he himself jumped like a frog to drink water from the river. Be not bound to anybody, any place, or thing.

20th April
Interrelated Fundamentals of Spiritual Life

Satyam or truth is the seed. Brahmacharya or celibacy is the root. Meditation is the shower. Santi or Peace is the flower. Moksha or emancipation is the fruit. Therefore speak the truth, practise celibacy, cultivate Santi and meditate regularly. You will surely attain the final emancipation or freedom from birth and death.

21st April
The Touchstone of Knowledge and Spirituality

Equal vision is the touchstone of knowledge. Unselfishness is the touchstone of virtue. Celibacy is the touchstone of ethics. Oneness is the touchstone of Self-realisation. Humility is the touchstone of devotion. Therefore, be unselfish, humble and pure. Develop equal vision. Be in tune with the Infinite.

22nd April
The Irreplaceable Precedents

Without Sadhana there is no meditation; without faith in the utterances of the sacred scriptures there is no improvement; without vigilance and alertness there is no progress in the spiritual path; without Guru there is no divine knowledge.

23rd April
Transformation of the Subconscious Life and Self-realisation this Moment

Beneath your conscious life there is a very wide region of subconscious life. Subconscious life is more powerful than your ordinary life of objective consciousness. Through the practice of Yoga you can modify, control and influence the subconscious plane. Bring about a complete transformation of the subconscious mind and attain superconscious experience or the fourth state, Turiya.

Can you serve like Florence Nightingale? Can you obey like a soldier in the battlefield? Can you be generous like Ranti Deva? Can you spend sleepless nights in devotion to the Lord, like Mira? Can you do Tapas like Dhruva? Can you stick to your convictions like Mansoor and Shams Tabriez? Can you be fearless like the sage who met Alexander the Great, on the banks of the Indus?

If you say Yes, you will have Self-realisation this very second. You will contact Avataras and full-blown Yogis this very second. First deserve, and then desire.

Chapter 11
THE SPIRITUAL PROGRESSIONS

24th April
The Irreligious and the Conscious Endeavour

The irreligious man also will reach God ultimately, but through a longer and more painful route, after a lot of experience of the miseries of this world. The religious-minded man will go to Him by the short cut and enjoy the bliss of God in this very birth. The sooner you become religious-minded, the sooner you will reach the Fountain-source of Bliss.

25th April
Feverish Hurry and Progressive Evolution

Spiritual growth is gradual. There is progressive evolution. You should not be in a feverish hurry to accomplish great Yogic feats or enter into Nirvikalpa Samadhi in two or three months. You will have to ascend the ladder of Yoga step by step. You will have to march in the spiritual path stage by stage.

26th April
Mechanism of Spiritual Unfoldment

Grow. Evolve. Expand. Develop pure Love Reflect. Meditate. Obtain Jnana. Have you unfolded the hidden treasures of spiritual consciousness latent in your heart? If yes, you have done well. Hail, hail to thee, Saumya!

Spiritualise all your activities. Let your eyes look with kindness, your tongue speak with sweetness, your hand touch with softness. Feed your mind with thoughts of God, your heart with purity, and your hands with selfless service. Remain soaked in remembrance of God.

27th April
Signs of Spiritual Progress

Growth in meditation, progress in Sadhana, and a closer approach to the Divine reveal themselves in the lightness of the body and mind, in the thinning out of the body-consciousness, in the loss of sex-attraction, in a distastefulness for worldly prosperity that the aspirant experiences. Contentment, unruffled state of mind, decrease in the excretions, sweet voice, eagerness and steadiness in the practice of meditation, desire to remain alone in a quiet room or to stay in seclusion, one-pointedness of mind, are some of the signs that indicate the advancement of the aspirant on the spiritual path.

28th April
Overmental Experience of the Thinker

The end of the Evolution of the Thinker is reached when the evolving mental life becomes, by expansion, identical with the all-including life, the universal Self. If, however, his thoughts and actions are directed exclusively towards personal and selfish ends, his mind contracts more and more and recedes more and more from the path of evolution. He should therefore think only such thoughts and do only such actions as may widen his mind. The mind has to expand until the limiting mind-covering, becoming very thin is torn asunder when the limitations of the Thinker ceasing to exist any longer, his Inner Self shines in his infinitude of existence, consciousness and bliss, for, it was only He, the only One and Real Self that was appearing till then to be enclosed in a covering made of mind-stuff.

29th April
Optimum Utilisation of Time

Those who want to become magnetic and dynamic personalities or prodigies should utilise every second to the best possible advantage and should try to grow mentally, morally and spiritually every second. Struggle hard. In spiritual path there is no falling back or resting even for a while. Even a little stagnation is sufficient to rust your spiritual being. A little lack of vigilance may cause a great downfall.

PART III

INTUITIONAL PLANES AND THE STRUCTURE OF THE LIFE DIVINE

Chapter 12
INTELLECTUAL ACROBATS AND THE SPIRITUAL SUPERMEN

30th April
Noetic Feats and Intensive Sadhana

Be it understood that he who has no Atma-Jnana, Self-knowledge and Experience, is a confirmed fool, even though he may be a learned person, a master of the six schools of Indian philosophy, even though he is a research scholar of Harward University with diplomas and degrees (M.A., Ph.D., D.Sc., D.Litt.) suffixed to his name. His intellect is still stony and barren. One may know by heart all the Upanishads, Brahma Sutras, the Bhagavadgita, the Veda Angas, the Smritis, the Western philosophy and contemporary psychology, yet there is no salvation for such a learned man without the realisation of his identity with Brahman through constant, intense meditation—not even in hundreds of millions of years. Therefore, practise meditation; hurry up, realise God now, here; all else is of little consequence.

1st May
Letters and Life

Mere study of Vichara-Sagara or Panchadasi cannot bring in the experience of pure Advaitic Consciousness. Vedantic gossipping, brilliant lectures on philosophy, and idle, dry talk on the Brahma Sutras and Upanishads cannot help a man in feeling the unity or oneness of life. There is no hope for such men to feel the Advaitic unity of Consciousness, unless they destroy ruthlessly all sorts of evils of mind and the heart; and start living the inward life.

2nd May
The Living Liberated Man

Not through matted locks, not through fiery lectures and erudition, not through exhibition of miracles does one attain perfection or Knowledge of the Self. He in whom the two currents of Raga-dvesha, ignorance of all kinds, egoism, lust and anger are destroyed in toto, is ever happy and he is Brahman, or the liberated Sage or Jivanmukta. When he is absorbed in Brahman, the Jivanmukta will not be able to work. But when he comes down from his full Brahmic consciousness owing to the force of Prarabdha and Vikshepa Sakti, he will pour forth his love at the cry of a suffering soul. He is the ocean of mercy, love and peace.

3rd May
The Occultist and the Jnani

An occultist learns through self-control and discipline to work on two planes at once, that is to be partly out of his body at the same time when he is working on the physical plane; so that even while he is busy writing, he may be doing other things with his astral body. When such is the case with an occultist, little need be said of a full-blown Jnani who is resting in his own Svarupa? He fixes himself on Brahman and uses his mind and body as his instruments, when he is doing Vyavahara. He has double consciousness: conscious of the world, he knows it to be a dream within himself, and conscious of the Brahman, he experiences Cosmic Consciousness. He knows what is going on in every mind.

4th May
The Solid World of the Sage

The sage in his flights of intuition ascends to that supramental region where he experiences the Divine Reality or the Absolute. The superconscious experience is very vivid, vital and vibrant. It is intensely real to the sage. He lives in it, moves in it and breathes in it. The intuitive experience-whole is grand, sublime and profound. The knowledge of God would have been lost to mankind but for the intuition and revelation of the seers.

5th May
The Vision of the Deathless Sage
In the crying babe, playing boy, fiery youth, puzzled woman, and the disillusioned old man—the sage perceives the same Divine Self. Outward form and peculiarity of nature do not matter with him. The apparent change which the worldly call death does not belong to the Divine Spirit within. Life continues beyond. Man sleeps with one encasement and wakes up after a short while with another encasement? Death has lost its dread for him. He has achieved the impossible, known the Unknowable—he has eluded the grasp of Death Itself! Like this sage, you too can conquer Death, and gain the Vision Divine. Seek for, and live dynamically in, the omnipresent Godhead.

6th May
The Voice of a Self-realised Sage
There is no paper on which to write the Nature of Truth. There is no pen which can dare write It. There is no person living who can express It. It merely is everything that is, and there ends the matter. Every effort to express Its nature is trying to kill its reality. Thou art that Great Being! Thou art this, thou art that! Thy glory knows no bounds. Thy power is indestructible. Thou art the most blessed, the Immortal, the Real. Realise thy real Nature through discrimination, dispassion and sacrifice of things earth-earthy.

7th May
Idle Talk and Transcendental Experience
Spiritual life is not mere idle talk. It is not mere sensation. It is actual living in the Atman. It is transcendental experience of unalloyed bliss. It is a life of fullness and perfection. He who leads a spiritual life is a centre of great spiritual force, a dynamic personality. He radiates peace, joy and bliss towards all; and those who come in contact with him will be highly inspired and elevated.

8th May
The Persisting Communities of Spiritual Individuals
The Grace of God is such that however universal be the sway of agnosticism, yet there remains always one class of people who refuse to succumb to the allurement of earthly things and live to strive for the attainment of a higher divine Ideal. These are the seekers, the monks in their monasteries, the wandering mendicants, and preachers, the recluses in their meditative isolation and the ascetics absorbed in penances. They are found even today not only in the East but also in the Western countries. There is no real difference between a Christian mystic and a Hindu saint. Their sayings never clash; their messages are essentially the same. They have always been a call to men to discover the Wisdom of the Self.

9th May
The Salt of the Earth
Great men are not those who speak much or run fast, but think deep and live rightly. Right thinking consists in the sinless attitude of the mind, and sin is belief in things that perish. They are great heroes who have gone to the other shore of the ocean of death and suffering and greater still are the saviours who offer the redeeming hand to the soul that writhes to have a glimpse of the Light that shall never flicker, that shall never fade away. The company of saints has a tremendous effect on the lives of true seekers. It lifts them up to the heights of sublimity, purity and spirituality. It affects even the rank materialists. Study the lives of saints; you are inspired at once. Remember their sayings; you are elevated immediately. Walk in their footsteps; you are freed from pain and sorrow.

10th May
The Great Superman of the East
The Bhagavad Gita is the Gospel of life, the scripture of humanity, and the life of Sri Krishna is the great commentary on it. Sri Krishna lived the life of a princely householder, teaching mankind that the Knowledge of the Absolute is not incompatible with practical activity in life. He is the form, as it were, taken by the great Truth that the universe is the manifestation of

Brahman. There was no end to the domestic troubles that Krishna had, no limit to the social and political disturbances and threatening situations in which Krishna was involved, no bound to his responsibility, and yet there was no match to his success, no equal to his shining example of the Life Perfect. Sri Krishna was a philosopher, a sage, a Yogi, and the statesman par excellence, who taught through example and precept the art of government, the way to maintain peace on earth.

Here are some valuable instructions of Sri Krishna to Uddhava. Sri Krishna says, "Give no attention to people who laugh in ridicule, forget the body, go beyond all sense of shame; fall prostrate on the ground and bow to all beings down even to the dog, the Chandala or the outcaste, the cow and the ass. See everything in Me and Me in everything. Cut off all sorts of attachments. Have perfect unswerving devotion to Me."

"Look upon this universe as a delusion, a play of the mind, now seen and the next moment destroyed, like a dream, and extremely inconsistent like the circle drawn by a firebrand (Alat Chakra). The threefold distinction of waking, dream and deep sleep which is caused by the transformation of Gunas, of the qualities of Nature, is Maya."

Chapter 13

INTUITIVE EXPERIENCE AND CONCEPTUAL KNOWLEDGE

11th May

Advaitic Wisdom and Human Reason

Wisdom is the perception of non-difference; ignorance is the reverse of it. Knowledge ascends by steps in sense, reason and intuition. Sensing is comparatively fragmentary false knowledge, and reason is midway between right and wrong and can be utilised to serve either end. Human knowledge ends with reason, and reason is always used to serve sense-knowledge. Logic that turns against intuition is untrustworthy. Reason is a hindrance to Self-realisation only when its logic gets perverted through selfish interest.

12th May
Intellect and the Nature of Intuition
Intellect gives the knowledge of external objects. Intellect is struggle. Intellect guesses, believes. Intellect is finite. Intellect is a product of Prakriti. Intuition is the eye of wisdom. Intuition is infallible. Intuition is a flash and an illumination. In intuition, time becomes Eternity. Therefore develop intuition.

13th May
The Intuitive Discernment and the Blindfold Efforts
Intuition, intuitive discernment, in fact is the only touchstone of philosophy. The method of intuition is the only method of discerning the Truth ultimately. Without developing intuition the intellectual man remains imperfect and blind to the Truth behind the appearances. In the light of developed intuition all other philosophies seem to be interesting tabletalks, funny essays, humorous attempts in the game called "Blindman's bluff."

14th May
The Definition of Intuition
Intuition is an active inner awareness of the immortal blissful Self within. It is the eye of wisdom through which the sage clearly discerns in everything the unseen Presence of the Reality. In Sanskrit terminology, it is called Divya Chakshus, Prajna Chakshus, Jnana Chakshus, through which the Yogi or the Sage experiences the supreme vision of the all-pervading Brahman. It corresponds to the Brahmakara Vritti of the Vedantins. It is the third spiritual eye of the Yogins.

15th May
Ancient Standards and Modern Measures
The age of the Upanishad was an age of intuitional perception. It was an age when intuitional experience was the guarantee of Truth. But the modern age is an age of questioning and criticism. Today the guarantee of truth is the test of sensual perception. That which man can perceive through his sense-organs or know through his intellect, that he accepts as the reality. That which the senses cannot perceive he rejects as unreliable.

Thus, many a precious factor in our ancient cultural heritage has been rejected and set aside as superstition.

16th May
Direct Perception and Conceptual Activity

Intuition is immediate knowledge in contrast with mediate knowledge. Intuition is the only way by which the Absolute can be realised and experienced in all its totality and integrality. These mortal limited senses and the finite intellect cannot comprehend the all-pervading Reality. Reason can give you only conceptual knowledge, and conceptual knowledge does not give you the knowledge of the Reality in its whole, in its totality, but it divides, fragmentises and breaks things into pieces.

Chapter 14
FOUNDATION OF SELF-REALISATION

17th May
Dynamic Movements of Spiritual Reflection

Amidst the din and boisterous bustle of worldly activities. there come moments of tranquillity and peace, when the mind for the time being, however short it may be, soars above the filthy worldly things and reflects on the higher problems of life, viz., "Whence? Where? Whither? Why of the universe? Who am I?" The sincere inquirer becomes serious and extends his reflections. He begins to search and understand the Truth. Discrimination dawns on him. He seeks Vairagya, concentration, meditation and purification of the mind and body and eventually attains the highest knowledge of the Self.

18th May
The Delphic Injunction

The greatest of the Greecian culture's contributions to the world of higher thought is the Delphic injunction, Know Thyself. It is around this Self-knowledge that all philosophies, monistic religions and spiritual sciences revolve. Self-knowledge is, in India, Self-Realisation. It is Self-Experience. Self-knowledge is not acquired through any intellectual or occult processes. It is knowledge by Identity. Those who have known themselves are those who have consciously contacted the Kingdom of Heaven present in the hearts of all.

19th May
The Two Axes of Self-Knowledge

Man cannot know himself save through meditation, through a deep dive into the calm chambers of the heart and a direct glance at the mirror of life within. To have a comprehensive understanding of what we are, we must impress on our mind the two facts, viz., the existence of the Eternal Reality, and the radical unity of all manifestations from star to mineral form, from inanimate nature to organised life. Every human being is a manifestation of the Lord; and, therefore, it is possible for everyone to become one with the Infinite. Reflection on the above truths of essential existence generates faith and conviction. Direct vision of the Reality supplants all vain arguments. Realisation of truth makes everything clear and self-explained.

20th May
Treasure Trove of Self-Knowledge

There are no works in all the world that are so thrilling, soul-stirring and inspiring as the Upanishads. The philosophy, taught by the Upanishads, has been the source of solace to many a great soul both in the East and the West. The Upanishads teach the philosophy of absolute unity, the glory of the essential Nature of man. They contain the sublime truths of Vedanta and practical hints and clues, which throw much light on the pathway of Self-Realisation.

21st May
The First Step and the Preceding Psychological Training

An enquiry after the subjective Centre, the Real Man, the metaphysical Entity that is lurking dormant in the heart of the intellectual, vital and physical encasements of every individual, is the first Step on the Path to the Life Divine. But the introspective cognition of the Self by the self becomes possible and flowers into the most effective operative power only after a certain necessary period of successful psychological training and discipline of the entire man.

22nd May
The Art of Introspection

You must learn the art of making the mind introspective or turned inward upon itself through the Yogic Kriya—Pratyahara (abstraction). Only then, can one be really happy. Those who know this practice, alone can be really peaceful. The mind cannot externalise itself and do any havoc now. It can be kept inside the Hridyaguha or the cave of the heart. You must starve the mind by Vairagya or dispassion and Tyaga or renunciation of desires, objects and egoism.

23rd May
Scientific Procedure of "Looking Within"

Just as the sun collects all its myriad rays and plunges beyond the horizon, the practitioner withdraws his mind from all his external senses into himself, like an octopus retracting its tentacles. It is a scientific centripetal movement, prior to the purposeful focussing of the full mind, which concentration implies. This can be likened to the circumference of a circle contracting into the centre. This practice renders the tendency of your nature 'inflowing' or Antarmukha. The individual gradually becomes an unmoved, undisturbed witness to. the play of outer phenomena.

24th May
Intellectual Discovery of the Light Divine

What gives you light, during the day? Sun. At night? Moon, stars and lamps. When there are no sun, moon, stars, what gives you light? Buddhi or the intellect. Who observes the workings of Buddhi and knows its defects and limitations? Aham: 'I': the self-luminous Light within. It is the inmost Principle in all, the Universal Ground. Do Sadhana and experience this Light of lights.

25th May
A Chain of Interiors
Mind is more internal than speech. Buddhi or intellect is more internal than mind. Ahamkara is more internal than Buddhi. Jiva Chaitanya Abhasa (reflected intelligence) is more internal than Ahamkara. Atman or Kutastha is more internal to Atman. It is Paripoorna or All-Full. This is your essential Nature. Realise this.

26th May
Reasoning Into the Substratum
Man is generally attracted by brilliant light, beauty, intelligence, varied colours and pleasant sounds. Do not be deceived by these fascinating objects and paltry things. Enquire within. What is the substratum for all things? There is the one Essence, the All-Beauty at the back of the mind and behind all objects of this seeming sense-universe. That Essence is all-full and self-contained. You are That Essence. Realise this.

27th May
Where Wisdom Dawns
Wisdom or Knowledge of the Self, Brahma-Jnana, never dawns upon the mind, which is filled with greed, anger lust and jealousy, which is under the control of desires and expectations and which is devoid of contentment. Wisdom dawns only in a pure and calm mind. Therefore, purify your mind and develop serenity.

28th May
Not an Act of Becoming But a Fact of Being
Self-realisation is not a process. It is not a becoming. It is pure being. It is not a new thing to be attained. The man of Self-realisation knows that he is the all-pervading Immortal Self. To know That is to be That. Self-realisation is direct intuitive perception of one's own innermost Self. Realise this mysterious, wonderful, all-blissful Self and move about happily.

29th May
The Persuasions of Self-Experience

The goal of life is the attainment of divine consciousness. This goal is the realisation that you are neither this perishable body nor that changing and finite mind, but you are all-pure ever free Atman. Remember always Ajo Nityah Sasvatoyam Purano: Unborn Eternal Permanent is this Ancient One. This is your real nature. You are not this little passing personality hooked on to a name and form. You are not Ramaswamy or Mukherji or Mehta or Matthew or Garde or Apte. You have only fallen into this little delusion by an accident through some passing cloud of ignorance. Awake and realise that you are Pure Atman.

Man is God in disguise who puts on a garb in fun, but quickly forgets his true identity. Desire drags him down. Discrimination lifts him up. God became man. Man will become God again. Man evolved is God. God involved is man. God in bondage is man, and man free from bondage is God. A deluded, ignorant man is worldly. A perfect man is God. God plus desire is man. Man minus desire is God. The most impious of men can, by earnestly devoting themselves to God, reach the highest bliss.

Truth is not outside you. It is within you. It dwells in the cave of your heart. You are a truth of God, a work of God, a will of God. You are unfettered, free, eternally free. You are Nityamukta Atman. Roar OM. Come out of the cage of flesh and roam about freely.

Chapter 15

THE PROCESSES OF SELF-KNOWLEDGE

30th May
The Psychic Ordeal Involved in Self-realisation

To realise the imperishable conscious Spirit, is the salvation of the individual, the endless supernal beatitude. Such a realisation is not given to all and sundry, it does not fall from the sky. The cost is very high, though it is open to all who are prepared for that. The price demanded is the very beloved self, the sacrifice of all that is dear and near. No tall talk, no excuse, no trick can help one in Self-realisation. It requires a conscious self-abandonment, an emptying of the self into an utter zero, a becoming totally non-existence as it were, to become truly existent.

31st May
The Primary Bases of Self-realisation

Self-realisation or an Experience of the Omnipresent Reality must be preceded by a preparatory peeping into the inner regions of our deeps, a heroic battling up our way to the very meaning and source of all life, a burning love and a consuming zeal for the attainment of the Divine Light and Grace; otherwise, one is sure to lose one's way in false paths and face defeat and disillusionment

1st June
Sadhana for Self-realisation

Analyse your thoughts. Scrutinise your motives. Remove selfishness. Calm the passions. Control the Indriyas. Destroy egoism. Serve and love all. Purify your heart. Cleanse the dross of mind. Hear and reflect. Concentrate and meditate. Attain Self-Realisation.

Put the Neti-neti doctrine of Vedanta, into daily practice. "Neti, neti" means "not this, not this". Say, "I am not this perishable body. I am not this mind. I am not this Life-force, Prana. I am not the senses." Try to identify yourself with the all-pervading Self. This practice culminates in the attainment of Self-realisation.

2nd June
The Method of Self-realisation

Turn the gaze, draw the Indriyas,
Still the mind, sharpen the intellect;
Chant OM with feeling, meditate on Atman!

An aspirant desirous of experiencing the Inner Self, turns his gaze within himself, withdraws the rays of his mind: the senses are drawn in as the limbs of a tortoise are drawn into the shell. The mental modifications are stopped. Buddhi is made to surrender itself at the feet of the Atman. Ego is emptied, so that his entire being might be filled by the light of the Self.

3rd June
Sequence of Merging

Merge your speech in the mind. Merge the mind in intellect. Merge the intellect in the cosmic intellect. Merge the cosmic intellect in the Unmanifest. Merge the Unmanifest in Pure Consciousness. This is self-withdrawl and self-expression; this is negation and affirmation; the negation of the personality and the affirmation of Universality and Omnipresence.

4th June
The Imperative Need

God-realisation is not a matter to be postponed till retirement. It is not a matter to be discussed in Lalbagh and Dalhousie Parks. It is a vital urgent need to be attended to immediately. A weak, emaciated and decrepit old body is not fit for Yoga Sadhana. Offer the prime of your youth to God, a rare flower of fresh fragrance.

Life is short. Time is fleeting. Obstacles are many. Cut the knot of Ignorance and drink the Nirvanic Bliss. Live well every day as if it is the last. Every moment is vitally important; every day is like turning of a new leaf. Waste not even half a second. Plunge yourself in Japa, meditation and service of humanity.

5th June
Attunement with the Divine

God, the supreme Almighty Spirit is the only Truth of life. Link yourself with Him through spiritual Sadhana. All suffering and sorrow is due to your losing touch with your Divine Source. To regain your contact with That Blissful One, you have been given this human body. The meaning of life is not to merely live as long as life lasts and then die when it ends. This is absurd. Life is intended purely for the attainment of Immortality and Eternal Bliss. Start your spiritual life now.

6th June
Precursory Condition for God-realisation

The Sadhaka should have burning Vairagya and Vichara, extreme earnestness and sincerity of purpose, for Darshan of God. He should show that intensity of feeling of the fish out of the water which flutters about for re-entry into it, of the man who runs for the firebrigade when his house is on fire, of the child in the river that shrieks for getting out, of the young wife who pines for meeting her husband who is expected to arrive from a foreign land after a long separation, of the person who wants the doctor for removal of foreign bodies from his eyes. Only then will the aspirant have the Vision of God, and gain the Experience Divine.

7th June
Prerequisites of a Perfect Life

To attain fellowship with other beings, to think in terms of everything that is around, to share in the feelings of the different breathing contents of the universe, in other words, to give freedom to your inner expressions and potentialities, to raise your self from the egoistic thinking, and to surrender the physical and the mental consciousness to a still higher unifying substance, is indeed the precondition of the truly happy and perfect life.

8th June
The Terminological Inexactitude

Desire for liberation is terminological inexactitude. Liberation means attainment of the state of Infinity. It already exists. It is our real nature. There can be no desire for a thing which is your very nature. All desires for progeny, wealth, for happiness in this world or in the next, and lastly even the desire for liberation, should be completely annihilated, and all actions guided by pure and disinterested will towards the goal.

Chapter 16
THE STRUCTURE OF THE LIFE DIVINE

9th June
Fitness for Life Divine

Just as the coloured water penetrates freely and nicely a piece of cloth when it is pure white so also the instructions of a sage can penetrate and settle down in the hearts of aspirants only when their minds are calm, when there are no desires for enjoyments and when the impurities of their minds are destroyed. That is the reason why an aspirant is expected to possess the qualifications of Viveka, Vairagya, Sama, Dama and Uparati before he practises hearing of Srutis, reflection and meditation. Discipline and purification of the mind and the Indriyas are the prerequisites of an aspirant in the path of Truth and Self-realisation.

10th June
Foundation of Divine Life

To be jealous is mean, to be selfish is ignoble, to be compassionate is divine, to be patient and enduring is manly, to be dispassionate is praiseworthy, and to be equanimous is laudable. Therefore eradicate jealousy and selfishness, and cultivate the divine virtues. Strive to be as compassionate as Buddha, as pure as Bhishma, as truthful as Harischandra, as brave as Bhima.

11th June
Integral Parts of the Life Divine

Divine Life is a synthesis of service, devotion and knowledge. It is not a dry philosophical doctrine. It is the Yoga of Synthesis which is eminently suited to the people of this age. It is practical religion. It enables you to converse with God daily, hourly, minute after minute. In such communion lies supreme goodness, eternal joy and immortality.

12th June
The Anatomy of Life Divine

Divine Life is the perfect life led according to the laws of the Divine Being. It is the Expression of the Real Essence of Existence. It is a life perfectly freed from the attractions of terrestrial egoism. It is the Life Immortal, the Ideal State of Perfection. Such a life has to be lived through a strenuous discipline and right moulding of the self of man.

13th June
When Cosmic Life Intervenes

When the heart is purified, the mind is naturally turned towards God. The aspirant is attracted towards God. Eventually he is absorbed in the Lord, through pure love, self-surrender and worship. The Bhakta now becomes a cosmic entity. He has one continuous life. He has cosmic life.

This cosmic life leads the aspirant into the Experience of the Timeless Reality In this experience there is neither darkness nor void. It is all-light. In it you become omniscient and omnipotent. You become *Sarvavid* or all-knower. You know the whole mystery of creation and gain eternal Bliss.

14th June
In the Realm of the Real

The goodness, the light, the pleasure and the beauty, of the world is not to be found there even in name. Even the splendour of the sun and the grandeur of the creator is superceded by the Absolute. That state is experienced when the senses ceases to work together with the mind and when the intellect does not move, and when there is nothing but Consciousness. When all desires that are lodged in the heart are liberated, then the mortal becomes Immortal. Here and now he attains Brahman.

PART IV
PATTERNS OF HUMAN GREATNESS

Chapter 17
CARDINAL PRINCIPLES OF GREATNESS

15th June
The Promises of Perseverance
The nerve that never relaxes, the eye that never blenches, the thought that never wanders—these are the masters of victory. Victory belongs to the most persevering. Perseverance gives power to weakness, and opens to poverty the wealth of the whole world. With steady perseverance, great difficulties come to an end. A man of perseverance never meets with failures. He always attains success. God is with those who persevere in spite of hindrances, discouragements and impossibilities. The tendency to persevere, to persist—it is this that distinguishes the strong soul from the weak. If you have perseverance you can do all that you wish.

16th June
Culture and the Prevailing Culture
Culture is not what it has unfortunately come to mean today: often diplomatic cunningness, hypocrisy, crookedness and immorality masquerade in the holy garb of culture! A cultured man has come to be regarded as one who wears a well-ironed suit, with a fashionable pipe adorning his smoke-emitting mouth, whose thoughts, actions and words are as correlated as those of an ego-intoxicated Gila Monster whose lips will utter sweet words while his heart is filled with loathsome thoughts of hatred, whose mouth would break into a grin while his heart frowns—whose polished manners hide the inner demon! True

culture is the process of conversion of the base animal nature of man, through the human, into the Divine.

17th June
Ahimsa: The Dynamic Spiritual Love

Positive all-embracing Love which Ahimsa means, a Compassion that is extended to all existences and all creation, forms the life-blood at once of the profoundest morality and of the highest spirituality: viewed from the sociological point of view, it forms the highest morality, and judged from individual standpoint, it means the dynamic intense spirituality. Even a feigning practice of Ahimsa by contemporary humanity would make world wars, social injustice and self-aggrandisement impossible, and convert this world into a happier and peaceful place to live in.

18th June
The Main Strand of Greatness

Magnanimity is loftiness of character or action. It is that elevation or dignity of soul which raises the possessor above revenge and makes him delight in acts of benevolence, which makes him disdain injustice and meanness and prompts him to sacrifice personal ease, interest and safety for the accomplishment of useful and noble objects. Magnanimity is generosity in sentiment or conduct towards others. It is exaltation above envious, cowardly, vindictive or selfish motives. A man of magnanimity is elevated in sentiment, scorns temptations, what is mean and base and despises earthly pomp and splendour.

19th June
The Importance of Manners

Good manners render a superior amiable, an equal agreeable and an inferior acceptable. They smooth distinctions, sweeten conversation, and make everyone in the company pleasant with himself. They produce good nature, mutual benevolence, soothe the fierce. 'Manners' is good behaviour or respectful deportment. Manners are the blossom of good sense and good feeling. A man of good manners is free from rudeness. He is well-behaved, complaisant, civil, courteous and polite. Pride, ill-nature, want of sense, arrogance, impatience are the great sources of ill-manners. Manners are minor morals.

20th June
Triune Aspect of the Twin Virtue

Selflessness and cosmic love are the very alpha and omega of spiritual life. They form the foundation of life divine, and their influence is felt throughout the superstructure. It would be quite true to say that these two virtues form the most essential prerequisites, the disciplines, the test of progress, the Supreme Attainment and its later manifestation. Selflessness and cosmic love are the Sadhana, the Sadhya and the Siddhi. They are the guiding lights of the Sadhaka, and the aura of the Siddha.

21st June
The Nature of Nobility

Nobility is that elevation of soul which comprehends bravery, generosity, magnanimity, intrepidity, and contempt of everything that dishonours character. Nobility is the state or quality of being noble in character as distinguished from selfishness, cowardice and meanness. It is dignity, grace of character, greatness of mind, magnanimity, excellence. The true standard of quality is in the mind: he who thinks nobly is really noble. Nobility is the finer portion of the mind and heart, linked to divinity.

22nd June
The Transmuting Power of Patience

Patience strengthens the spirit, sweetness the temper, stifles anger, develops the will-force, extinguishes jealousy, subdues pride, controls the organ of speech, restrains the hand. In patience there is quiet endurance or forbearance under distress, pain, injury, insult, suspense, calamity, provocation. He has endurance without murmuring or fretfulness or retaliation. Patience is a specific remedy for the control of anger. It is the soul of peace. It is genius.

23rd June
The Meaning of Manliness

'Manly' refers to all the qualities and traits worthy of a man. Manliness is the quality of soul which frankly accepts all conditions in human life and makes it a point of honour not to be dismayed or wearied by them, it is more than courage. We speak of manly gentleness or tenderness,—such as firmness, bravery, undaunted spirit, dignified nature, nobility and stateliness. Manliness is freedom from childishness, boyishness, and womanishness.

24th June
Blessed Are the Meek

Meekness is gentleness of disposition, that low, sweet root from which all divine virtues shoot up. Meekness is the essence of true religion, the fundamental virtue of a saint. It is the root, the mother, the nurse, of all virtues. Meekness is the noblest self-denial. It is abstinence from self-love and self-conceit. It abounds in goodwill, excludes revenge, irritability, morbid sensitiveness. Meekness is submission to Divine Will. God delights to dwell in the hearts of the meek.

25th June
The Quintessence of Courtesy

Courtesy sweetens and ennobles life. It makes smooth the road of life, like grace and beauty. It opens the door and allows the stranger into the house. It enlivens the hearts of guests and visitors. A man of courtesy is a man of fine and polished manners. All people love him. Courtesy charms at first sight and leads on to great intimacy and friendship. Let your courtesy be artless, continuous and uniform.

26th June
The Good and Not Good

To be abstemious in diet is good; but trying to live on leaves is not good. To take care of the body is good: but to be attached to the body is not good. To live in seclusion is good; but to become Tamasic is not good. To be frank is good; but to expose another's secrets and faults is not good. May the reader obtain the Supreme Good.

27th June
Good Life and God-Life

Good conduct is the root of material and spiritual prosperity. It increases fame, prolongs life, ends evils, and brings continued happiness. It is good conduct that begets virtue. And out of good life comes God-life. Goodness is the threshold to Godliness. Divine Life is a good life plus an inner awareness of the Nature of the Self, Atman. Having conscientiously endeavoured to lead a good and honest life, therefore, you have won half the battle.

28th June
Pen-Picture of an Honest Man

An honest man is characterised by openness, genuineness or sincerity. He is faithful, sincere, straightforward, true, trustworthy, upright. He is always disposed to act with careful regard for the rights of others, especially in matters of business or property. He scrupulously observes the dictates of a personal honour that is higher than any demands of mercantile law or public opinion and will do nothing unworthy of his own inherent nobility of soul. No success in Yoga, no spiritual progress is possible without honesty.

29th June
The Adverbial Guides

Eat sparingly. Breathe deeply. Talk kindly. Work energetically. Think usefully. Stick resolutely. Act rightly. Apply tenaciously. Behave properly. Speak politely. Pray wholeheartedly. Endure courageously. Persevere patiently. Concentrate singlemindedly. Meditate seriously. Realise quickly.

If you want to progress rapidly in Sadhana, talk a little, mix a little, walk a little. Much talking will cause distraction of the mind; much mixing will cause disturbance in the mind; much walking causes exhaustion and weakness. Pursue Sadhana earnestly.

30th June
Nature's Comment on Jesus' Command
Dense rain clouds sail in majestic langour, heavy with hidden rain. Tall mountains arrogantly bar their way, and offer granite opposition. Enfolding them in their cooling embrace the clouds pour forth all their treasured waters over the bosom of their foe. Oh, how beautifully do they teach! To him who smiteth thee on thy left cheek turn thy right cheek too. If a man taketh away thy cap give him thy coat also. Love him that hateth thee. Bless him that curseth thee.

1st July
Praise and Censure: An Appraisement
They blame him who is a bachelor, they blame him who has married, they also blame him who has embraced Sannyasa. There is no one on earth who is not blamed. Blame and praise are vibrations in the air. Therefore, be above blame and praise and be happy.

In sticking to the path of righteousness and spiritual life, you will face mockery, misunderstanding and persecution. Therefore, the cultivation of forbearance, meekness of spirit, calm endurance, and spirit of forgiveness are of great importance. Uphold virtue at any cost; for its sake, hear any calumny. Return good for evil.

2nd July
Spiritual Self-enrichment
Everything will end well for those who are truthful and sincere and who rely on God. Throw your burden on Him and rest peacefully for ever. Do not bother about domestic affairs. Forget all about the past. He who takes care of the frog within the strata of rock will surely take care of all His creation. Increase your Japa and spend more time in sitting alone. This is your supreme wealth.

3rd July
Modesty: The Best of Moral Excellences

Modesty is the absence of all tendency to overestimate oneself. It is freedom from excess, exaggeration or extravagance. It is decent reserve or propriety of manner or speech. It is purity of thought, character, feeling or conduct. It is becoming behaviour, humility, a discerning grace. It is a beautiful setting to the diamond of talent and genius. It is the greatest ornament of an illustrious life. It is the appendage of sobriety. The speech of a modest man is inspiring, and elevating. It touches your heart, breathes love and wisdom, gives lustre to truth. A modest man who is unostentatious, unassuming, unpretentious, is respected by all. He wins the hearts of all.

However, one cannot attain to perfection merely by the practice of modesty, by mere goodness, by pursuit of virtues. One has to meditate intensely on the Divine ideal, with the help of such virtues as humility, modesty, purity. Virtue and morality act as auxiliaries to meditation and final mergence of the individual in the Supreme.

All ethics have, as their aim, the realisation of the Self. Ethics leads to restraint of the lower self and thereby the mind is calmed. Through calmness of the mind discrimination dawns, and one knows the Self, realises God, in a short time.

Chapter 18
WILL-POWER AND THE FORMATION OF PERSONALITY

4th July
Personality and Control of Thoughts

A sublime thought elevates the mind and expands the heart; a base thought excites the mind and renders the feelings morbid and dark. Those who have even a little control over their thoughts and speech will have a calm, serene, beautiful, charming face, a sweet voice and their eyes will turn brilliant and lustrous.

5th July
Personality and Physical Features

Personality includes a man's character, intelligence, noble qualities, moral excellences, noble conduct, intellectual attainments, certain striking characteristics, sweet, powerful voice, and so on. All these and many more put things together constitute the personality of a man. Mere physical form or characteristics do not make up the personality. A fully blown Yogi or Jnani is the greatest personality in the world. He may be of a small status and even ugly, clad in rags; and yet he is a mighty personality a great Mahatma. A man who has attained ethical perfection by the continued practice of right conduct has also got a magnetic personality. He can influence millions.

6th July
Prana, Power and Personality

The Prana is related to the Mind and through Mind to Will and through will to the Individual soul and through this to the Supreme Being. If you know how to control the little waves of Prana working through the mind, then the secret of subjugating Universal Prana will be known to you. The Yogi who becomes an expert in the Knowledge of this secret, will have no fear from any power, because he has mastery over all the manifestations of Power in the universe. What is commonly known as Power and personality are nothing more than the natural capacity of a person to wield his Prana.

7th July
The Shaping of Personality

Mould your character. Behave properly. Develop sympathy, affection, benevolence, tolerance and humility. Come out of the centre of your small narrow egoistic circle and have a broad vision. Speak gently and sweetly in a courteous manner. Eradicate undesirable thoughts and desires.

8th July
Ill-health: A Myth
Ill-health is a myth. It does not exist beyond the range of the physical and mental sheaths. The body and mind alone are subject to disease. The Atman, your true Self is beyond these and therefore eternally free from diseases and death. During illness, detach yourself from the body. Connect the mind with the Atman. "As you think, so do you become!" Therefore, assert. "All health I am OM OM OM." Disease will take to its heels.

9th July
Nature, Status and Power of Will
Will is the dynamic soul-force. When it operates all the mental powers such as the power of judgment, power of memory, power of grasping, power of conversation, reasoning power, power of discrimination, power of reflection and inference—all these come into instant play. Will is the king of mental powers. When rendered pure and irresistible, will can work wonders. Will becomes impure and weak through vulgar passions, love of pleasures and desires. Fewer the desires, the stronger the will. When sexual energy, the muscular energy, anger, etc., are all transmuted into the will-force they are controlled. There is nothing impossible on earth for a man of strong will-power.

10th July
Aids to the Development of Will-Power
Every temptation resisted, every sensual thought repressed, every harsh word withheld, every noble aspiration encouraged, helps you to develop your will-power or Soul-force and takes you nearer and nearer to the Goal. Sincerity in Sadhana is the key to success. With strong feeling, repeat mentally: "My will is powerful, pure, and irresistible. OM OM OM. I can do everything through my will. OM OM OM. I have an invincible will. OM OM OM."

11th July
The Harvest of a Controlled Desire

When you give up an old habit of drinking coffee, you have controlled to a certain extent the sense of taste, destroyed one Vasana, and have eliminated the craving for it. As there is freedom from the efforts to procure coffee and also from the habit of taking it, you will gain some peace. The energy involved in the hankering for coffee, and which was agitating you, will now be converted into the power of will. By this conquest over, you gain will-power; and if you conquer some fifteen such desires, your will-power will fifteen times be stronger and more powerful. And this conquest, by imparting strength to the will, will help you conquer other desires, too.

12th July
The Signs of Growing Will

Unruffled state of the mind, poise, cheerfulness, inner strength, capacity to turn out difficult works, success in all undertakings, power to influence people, a magnetic and dynamic personality; magnetic aura on the face, sparkling eyes, steady gaze, powerful voice, a magnanimous gait, unyielding nature, fearlessness, etc., are some of the signs or symptoms that indicate that one's 'will' is growing.

The source of all life, the source of all knowledge, is Atman, your innermost Self. This Atman or supreme Soul is transcendent, inexpressible, uninferable, unthinkable, indescribable, the ever-peaceful, all-blissful. It is Omnipotent; the more you reflect upon its infinite Strength, and the more you are conscious of this inner Power of the Infinite in you, the greater is your will-power.

You should have real and intense thirst to realise your inner Self, the Godhead within you. Then your will-power increases hundredfold and dissolves all obstacles.

Purity of heart and concentration greatly increase will-power. The more is the mind fixed on God the more is the strength you acquire. More concentration means more energy and more will-power.

Chapter 19
SELF-DEVELOPMENT AND THE SPIRIT OF SELFLESS SERVICE

13th July
Purity of Mind and Selfless Service

Karma Yoga prepares the mind for the reception of Light and Knowledge. It expands the heart and breaks all the barriers that stand in the way of oneness or unity. Karma Yoga is an effective Sadhana for Chitta Suddhi or purity of the mind-stuff and the heart. Therefore do selfless service constantly. Take delight in service.

The more the energy you spend in elevating and serving others, the more the divine energy which will flow to you. Work with the awareness of being pulled by the Cosmic Will. You will have more strength, less vanity. You will not be bound, as there will be no 'mine-ness'.

14th July
Fields for Cultivating Selflessness

Different forms of social service, personal service to the sick and the suffering, negation of the superiority complex through self-denial, menial labour and fraternisation with those whom the society will not grant equality, are all different fields for cultivating selflessness and breaking open the barrier of separateness.

15th July
Definition of a Selfish Action

All selfish actions are immoral. What, then, is selfish action? It is an action which is intended to bring satisfaction to the senses and the ego of one's own individual being without any intention to overcome the desires of the senses and the ego. In addition to those positive indulgences, immoral action includes other acts like causing harm, practising falsehood and committing theft, either in thought or word or deed, passion, anger, greed, pride and jealousy are immoral actions.

16th July
Evils of Selfishness
Selfishnees is the source of all vices. A selfish man injures others, robs them of their property and does many sinful actions to satisfy his selfishness. Selfishness constricts the heart. A selfish man has neither scruples nor character. Peace of mind is unknown to him. It is selfishness that prompts a man to do evil acts.

17th July
Social Scavengery
Mere philanthropic work occasioned by either sympathy or gain of personal fame, without devotion and knowledge is nothing more than social scavengering. It is not Yoga. The whole heart, mind, intellect must be dedicated to service: this is Isvararpana or Yoga. Remember, it is the mental attitude or Bhava that does immense good. Feel that you are an instrument in the hands of God. It is through the light provided by the self-effulgent Lord within you that you are able to work. Feel this every moment of your life. Act and serve as a trustee, not as an owner or proprietor. You will be free from Karma, you will not be bound to action as there will be no "mine-ness".

18th July
Spiritual Triads for Practice
Three things to love: desire for liberation, company of the wise and selfless service; three things to despise: miserliness, cruelty and petty-mindedness; three things to admire: generosity, courage and nobility; three things to respect: Guru, renunciation and discrimination; three things to control: tongue, temper and tossing of the mind.

19th July
Censoriousness and Self-reformation

If you spend even a fraction of the time that you waste, in finding your own faults, you would have become a great saint by this time. Why do you care for the faults of others? Purify yourself first. Improve yourself first. Reform yourself first. Wash the impurities of your own mind. He who applies himself diligently to his spiritual practices cannot find even a single second to look into the affairs of others.

20th July
The Graded Levels of Spiritual Growth

Desires are incentive to action. Transmute first unholy desires into holy desires. Action leads to experience. Experience results in the growth of the soul. Soul-growth unfolds all the beauty and glory of the latent spiritual powers which make you free and perfect. Distill out of your experience that divine Essence of serenity, poise and pure love; and this, in its turn, will make you a godman.

21st July
The Three-Pronged Method

When an evil thought harasses the mind, the best method of conquering it is by ignoring it. How can we ignore an evil thought? By forgetting it. How can we forget? By not indulging in it again, and also by not brooding over it. How can we prevent the mind from indulging in it again or brooding over it? By thinking of something very interesting, something sublime and inspiring. Ignoring, Forgetting, Thinking, of something inspiring,—these three constitute the great Sadhana for establishing mastery over evil thoughts.

22nd July
Mental Power Through Controlled Thoughts

Uncontrolled thoughts are the roots of all evils. The more the thoughts are restrained, the more is the mind concentrated and consequently the more does it gain in strength and power. It demands patient work to destroy mean and base thoughts: but the entertainment of sublime thoughts is the easiest and rapid method of destroying base thoughts. Ignorant of the laws of thought, the worldly-minded individual falls a prey to all sorts of thoughts, thoughts of hatred, anger, revenge, lust and grows very weak-willed. The best method of gaining mental power is by entertaining sublime, noble and good thoughts and through their aid controlling the dissipative, distractive, diversifying worldly, and base thoughts.

Chapter 20

THE TRANSCENDENTAL REACHES OF BLESSEDNESS

23rd July
Contentions of Contrary Temperaments

The view that everything in nature and in the history of mankind is ordained for the best, the order of things in the universe being adapted to produce the highest good, enables the optimist to see an opportunity in every difficulty, to discover a bright side to every situation, to adopt a hopeful and confident state of mind, and to get the best of life and make the best of circumstances. The doctrine that the world and human life are essentially evil, that this is the worst possible world, condemns the gloomy and depressed pessimist to see a difficulty in every opportunity, to believe that everything is tending to the worst, to be disposed to take a despairing view of life, to anticipate failure or misfortune. The sanguine temperament of the optimist shows that the accident is not as terrible as you feared; the hill is not so steep as you thought before you began climbing; the difficulty is not as great as you expected, and that the things come out better than you hope. The pessimist has a temper of mind that looks to the darker side of things and paints the darkness exaggeratedly far darker than what it is, and tends to maintain that things are bad rather than good, worse rather than bad. Maintain faith in yourself and look up; succeed in life; become a powerful optimist; rejoice in the all-pervading Divinity.

24th July
The Factor that Determines Happiness

Man today has totally become a slave of artificial gadgets and synthetic products even in matters of food, personal health and every little matter of day-to-day life. He is a rag doll propped up by a thousand scientific aids and devices. The measure of man's happiness is in proportion to his victory over environment. The less you depend upon other things, the greater your happiness. Depend upon outside objects for your satisfaction; then misery is the result.

25th July
The Experience of Peace

Peace is within. Search for peace within the chambers of your own heart, through one pointed concentration and meditation. If you do not find peace there, you will not find it anywhere else. All unhealthy desires cause distractions of various kinds, and are therefore enemies of Peace. Give up all cravings, egoism, and unnatural longings. The man who is endowed with supreme faith in the Divine Principle of God and who has mastery over his senses quickly gets the Highest Peace. The one aim of life is the attainment of peace and not achievement of power, name, fame and wealth.

26th July
Peace of Mind

Don't grieve at the unkind words of the world. Is it possible to please the people? There are so many tongues, so many talks, so many opinions, so many remarks. This world is a strange mixture of the forces of Sattva, Rajas and Tamas. Tamasic people are in abundance; and, it is their second nature to find fault and pronounce unnecessary criticism. They experience the world through their primitive emotions; their judgment is prejudiced; their natures are small; they are a prey to the sins of sense and perversions of will; they are more governed by ignorance and egoism than by intelligence and light. Therefore, follow the dictates of your own conscience and the promptings of your soul. If you are satisfied, the whole world must be satisfied.

27th July
The Conquest of Happiness

Do not jeer at any one. Do not frown at anybody. Restrain all your senses. Be cheerful always. Do not look back: make steady progress on the path of goodness. Divest yourself of all desire and wrath. Cast off pride. Turn your gaze inwards. Contemplate. You will enjoy true happiness.

28th July
Peace of the Inner Self

Peace is absolute serenity and tranquility, wherein all the whims and fancies, daydreaming and imaginations, moods and impulses, emotions and instincts cease to operate entirely and the individual soul rests in its own native, pristine glory in an unruffled state. It is not, of course, the temporary condition of mental quietude which worldly people speak of in common parlance when they retire for a short time to a solitary bungalow in a forest for a little rest. Peace is the realm of infinite bliss and eternal Sunshine, where cares, worries, anxieties and fears which torment the soul, dare not enter; where all distinctions of caste, creed and colour vanish altogether in the one embrace of Divine Love and where desires and cravings find their full satiety.

29th July
Empirical Sources of Blessedness

Eat sparingly, breathe deeply, talk kindly, work energetically, bathe thoroughly and have a long life. Cultivate a melting heart, the giving hand, the kindly speech, the life of service, equal vision and impartial attitude. Your life will indeed be blessed.

Out of pain comes the philosophy of "Who am I?"; out of suffering comes endurance: out of service a pure, compassionate heart; out of adversity the strength of will; out of faith the final beatitude; and out of meditation oneness with the Infinite.

PART V

THE EVOLUTIONARY AIMS AND THE TECHNIQUES OF SPIRITUAL PERFECTION

Chapter 21

THE ESSENTIALS AND THE EVOLUTIONARY AIMS OF LIFE

30th July

Godhead: the Objective of Aspiration

Know that you seek, and then seek. See you not that what you pursue here fails to give you what you truly seek and recedes like a mirage? Nothing on earth can give you supreme joy, everlasting happiness, unadulterated bliss. Youth fades like the evening flower, strength vanishes like the rent cloud, the beauty of the body quickly gives way to the ugly death! Your pleasure-centres mock at you, for you have mistaken pain for happiness, night for day, mirage for water! The real goal of your aspiration, the true object that you seek, the sole purpose for which you live your life here, is the realisation of the Imperishable Bliss of the Godhead within.

31st July

The Self-exceeding Aims Inherent in Life

Final emancipation through the realisation of union of the Jivatman and the Paramatman alone is the goal; and this can be achieved by constant strenuous Sadhana. Pursuit of any other end is fraught with pain and horror of rebirth. A peaceful life comes through proper understanding of God, world and Jiva; a peaceful death is ensured by a clear conscience where shines the knowledge of the Immortal Self.

1st August
The Essentials of Life
The salt of life is selfless service. The bread of life is universal love. The water of life is purity. The sweetness of life is devotion. The fragrance of life is generosity. The pivot of life is meditation. The goal of life is Self-realisation. Therefore, serve, love, be pure and generous. Meditate and realise.

2nd August
Lessons in the School of Life
Life on earth is a school of wisdom and realisation of the Self. God is the unseen teacher who, through his great Sons, through nature herself, teaches man the secret and the source of the attainment of Life Immortal. Thus Life abounds with Lessons. He who heeds them, heads toward Freedom and Light; he who neglects, dooms himself in darkness.

The field of life is a great training centre. Individuals pass through different phases only to learn more and more and get wiser. Be, therefore, receptive and always keep the goal before you. To a really good life bitterness does not belong; here malice is unknown, fear exists not, and courage, peace and happiness ever abide.

3rd August
Is Life Evil?
Life as such is not an evil. But the evil consists in the delusion and the blind attachments in which life is involved, and the danger to while life leads man, viz., getting into worse states through ignorance than he is at any one time. Life free from desires or passions of all kinds is not evil. It is not escape from the world, but freedom from worldliness that is necessary.

4th August
Meaning of the Absolute in Actual Life
The indivisible, absolute and conscious nature of the Reality signifies that life on earth should be lived according to the rigid laws of dispassion towards external existence and active awareness of the Self as the unlimited being. It also shows that

all forms of physical and even intellectual indulgence are deviations from the eternal truth and that every desire for objectivation of consciousness is suicidal in the real sense. The good life which is in conformity with the nature of Truth should be, therefore, free from the oppressions of hatred and falsehood in all their forms of manifestation. The righteous life should be lived with mental peace, self-restraint, absence of agitative activity, fortitude, faith in Truth and concentration of mental consciousness.

5th August
The Wisdom of Life

Improper action, thoughtless action without discrimination gives rise to all miseries. To get freedom from misery, the noble path of virtue, Sadachara is the royal way. Let purity pervade your inner motives and outer conduct. Be loving and charitable in your opinion of men and things and also in all your dealings with others.

6th August
The Hindu View of Life

Life, the Hindu knows, is a war between the brute earth and the Heavenly Spirit, between the instincts and the intellect, between the forces of the Devil, all that is undesirable and the powers of God. Life is a steady growth; a progressive evolution characterises it. This earth-arena is a field of self-development. The perception of the one Life Principle or God in all, the merging of the personal soul in the Self of all creatures, great and small, says the Hindu, is the ultimate meaning and end of life.

7th August
The Chaotic Nature of Worldly Life

Worldly life is chaotic and fragmentary. It is full of noise, troubles, unrest, agitation and tribulations. A worldly man, though very wealthy and extremely intelligent, though holding a very high position, rank or status in society is a spiritual bankrupt. He lacks the beauty of holiness, the divine poise, the sense of absolute security, the grace and light of an enlightened soul.

Worldly life is characterised by appalling ignorance, disharmony and by a thousand forms of sorrow.

Life in God is free from sorrow and pain. It is full, rich, perfect, and independent. It is full of wisdom and eternal bliss. Live in God, in the inner Divine Being.

8th August
The Rich Expansive Life

Isavasyamidam Sarvam: Every content of the universe is throbbing with the Life of the Lord. Smile with the flowers and the green grass. Smile with the shrubs, fern and twigs. Develop friendship with all neighbours, dogs, cats, cows, human beings, trees in fact, with all nature's creations. You will have a perfect and rich life.

9th August
Trans-empirical Passages of Life

Life is a journey from impurity to purity, from hatred to cosmic love, from death to immortality, from imperfection to perfection, from slavery to freedom, from diversity to unity, from ignorance to eternal wisdom, from pain to eternal bliss, from weakness to infinite strength. Let every thought take you nearer to the Lord every act further your evolution.

10th August
Significance of Life and Death

Life is a scene where the individual puts on the dress of the form of a certain amount of desires which can be fulfilled in the special environment afforded by it, and death is the time when the individual goes behind the screen and puts on a new dress to appear in another scene of life in order to fulfil another quality of desires which cannot find the required atmosphere for fruition in the present life, but demand a fresh suitable environment. When properly understood neither of them is dreadful.

11th August
Integral View of Phenomenal Existence

Life on earth is not self-sufficient and, hence, there is a perpetual flux of states to reach other states of superior knowledge and happiness. Life in this world and this body is only a preparation, a step for the higher life. That which we see and hear of is not the all; the Real is beyond this. To reach the Real the present life acts as a ladder, a field of activity which directs the individual to realise the exalted Life Divine. The sense of values in life is judged by the standard of the incorruptible law of the inner Being which is the Self of all and not by the objective worth of things. Dealings with one another are justified only so long as they do not deviate from the eternal law of the spiritual Nature. Neither social welfare nor national betterment is possible by forgetting the essential Substance.

12th August
Aims and Ideals

To raise the fallen, to lead the blind, to share what I have with others, to bring solace to the afflicted, to cheer up the suffering are my ideals. To have perfect faith in God, to love my neighbour as my own Self, to love God with all my heart and soul, to protect cows, animals, women, and children are my aims. My watchword is Love. My goal is Sahaja Samadhi Avastha or natural, continuous, superconscious state.

Chapter 22

THE ASPIRANT AND THE INNATE IMPETUS TOWARDS THE INFINITE

13th August
The Restless Quest

The human soul, being in fact a part and parcel of the Infinite Existence, is in its essential nature identical with it. Being set awhirling in this cycle of the world-process, veiled from the knowledge of its essential Divinity and its Consciousness severely limited by the encasing sheaths of Matter, the Jiva ever seeks to put an end to this separation, limitation and the senses of incompleteness that it feels. Through successive incarnations, its life constitutes a constant reaching forth towards its Primal Abode of Infinite, Immortal Blissful Existence and until that state is attained, each centre of individualised Ego-consciousness will keep us this restless quest on the upward path of evolution. Through every moment Humanity as a whole is inevitably being drawn up towards that Ideal State of Perfect Existence.

14th August
Symptoms of Spiritual Adolescence

Man seeks in the accomplishment of ambitions projects the happiness that he feels he is in need of. But he finds that worldly greatness when secured, is a delusion and a snare; he doubtless does not find any happiness or peace in it. He gets degrees, diplomas, titles, honour, power, name, fame; he marries; he begets children; in short, he gets all that he supposes would give him happiness. But he finds no rest. Pious men, saints and sages declare that this restlessness of every man—this state of discontent, dissatisfaction and uncomfortableness, of being ill at ease with himself and his surroundings is solely due to the loss of the companionship with the infinite Reality, and an occult urge towards it.

15th August
The Divine Discontent

Spiritual hunger means thirst for God's Darshan. Spiritual hunger is the ultimate meaning of every activity in life. The dissatisfaction and the necessities of the life show that everyone, unconsciously, does suffer from spiritual hunger and it is not appeased until the Spirit within is realised. Without this divine discontent there is no real progress.

Spiritual hunger is the ultimate meaning of every activity in life. The dissatisfaction and restlessness that remain even after obtaining all the necessities of life show that everyone, consciously or unconsciously, does suffer from spiritual hunger, and it is not appeased until the Spirit within is realised. Without this divine discontent there is no real progress.

16th August
The Best-Qualified Aspirant

The Uttama Adhikari, who is, ever ardent, silent and serene due to the dawn of proper knowledge, ever the same among the diverse men of the world, undisturbed by the distracted activities of the workaday world, calm and peaceful, withdrawn himself from the bustle of life, unmindful of what is happening on earth, disinterested either in this or that, indifferent to the pleasures of a so-called successful life,—that is really fit indeed to receive the ultimate Wisdom of the Lord and the Truth. Even if there is the slightest desire lurking inside other than for the realisation of the Divine, that person will not be able to comprehend the true import of the Upanishadic teachings or the instruction by the spiritual teacher. He will have thousand doubts and distractions in the mind that make impossible all spiritual activity.

17th August
The Wrestle Against Finitude

Note how Vairagya arises in the mind. The transitory and perishable nature of all things creates a sort of disgust in all minds, and in proportion to the depth and subtlety of nature, this reaction from the world works more or less powerfully in the mind of every individual. An irresistible feeling arises in our mind, viz., that the finite can never satisfy the Infinite within us, that the changing and perishable cannot satisfy the changeless and deathless nature of ours. When you are fully aware of the magnitude of human sufferings in this miserable, relative world, you will naturally begin to discriminate between what is real and what is unreal.

18th August
The Theocentric Vision

That man who, living in the midst of temptations of the world disciplines his mind by devotional exercises is the true hero. The true hero can look on any direction he chooses while carrying a heavy burden on his head. Similarly, the perfect man whose mind is thoroughly disciplined has his eyes constantly directed towards God even when he is weighed down by the burden of worldly duties.

19th August
Summits Beyond Summits

Never rest contented with a little achievement or success in the path, with a little serenity of mind, a little one-pointedness of mind, some vision of angels or Siddhis, a little faculty of thought reading. There are still higher summits to ascend, higher regions to climb. Continue the spiritual practice.

Some aspirants leave Sadhana after some time. They expect great fruits quickly. They expect many Siddhis within a short time. When they do not get some, they give up the Sadhana. There are several ranges of consciousness between the ordinary human consciousness and the supraconsciousness of Brahman. Different veils have to be torn down on the way; many lower centres have to be opened up; many hurdles have to be crossed over before the final goal is reached.

When you are established in the highest Nirvikalpa Samadhi, when you have reached the final goal, you have nothing to see, nothing to hear, nothing to smell, nothing to feel. You have no body-consciousness. You have full Brahmic Consciousness. There is nothing but the Self. It is a grand experience; you will be struck with awe and wonder. You have simultaneous knowledge now. Past and future are blended into the eternal present. Everything is "now". Everything is "here". You have gone beyond time and space.

Chapter 23

MAN: HIS INHERITANCE AND HIS DESTINY

20th August

Metaphysical Significance of Man—I

The saying that man is the measure of all things is perfectly true. Man is a many-levelled being and has various sheaths which conceal his real personality. He may identify himself with the gross physical body and look to its needs as an animal does, or he may identify himself with the self-conscious reason, or he may feel his oneness with his Real Self which is the eternal witness of both. The vital aims, however valuable they may be in their own place, cannot take control of the spiritual being for a long time without complete disorder to one's personality. In the modern man self-conscious intellect, with all its natural limitations takes the highest place, and suicidal scepticism is the result.

21st August
Metaphysical Significance of Man—II
Intellect can move only in a vicious circle of possibilities. It hovers round an object: deeper, it can never go. It cannot enter into, and be one with it; and be it noted, without complete identity, knowledge is impossible. Intellect accepts the evidence of the senses and the result of inference, but it rejects as spurious the deepest subjective intuitions. Profound insight tells us that there is something more in man than is apparent in his ordinary consciousness; something which originates all thoughts and emotions, a finer spiritual presence which keeps him ever dissatisfied with mere earthly pursuits. The doctrine that the ordinary condition of man is not his final state, that he has a deeper self, an immortal Spirit, a light that can never be extinguished, has the longest, highest intellectual ancestry.

22nd August
Metaphysical Significance of Man—III
All the greatest thinkers of the world unite in asking us to know this Self. While our bodily organisation undergoes change every moment, while our thoughts gather like clouds in the sky and disperse again, the real Self is never lost. It is all-pervading though distinct from all. It is the source of the sense of identity through numerous transformations. It remains itself though it sees ,all things. It is the one constant thing which remains unchanged in the multiple activities of the universe. Our limited personality is conscious only by fits and starts. There are large gaps in it. Even if death overtakes a man, the seer in him cannot die.

23rd August
Metaphysical Significance of Man—IV
Nothing on the objective side can touch the subject. This ever-persisting Self which is the Eternal Subject, is not capable of proof, nor does it need any. It is Self-proved. It is the basic substratum of every act of knowledge, and vivifies every organ and faculty. This universal Self becomes confused with the empirical self owing to mental impurities. When we break through the ring of the smoke round the Self, unwrap the sheaths which

cover it, we achieve here and now, in the physical body, the destiny of our being. The "I", the "Atman" which is infinitely simple, is a trinity of transcendent Reality, Awareness and Freedom.

24th August
An Integral Study of Man

Man is not merely a biological phenomenon. There is in him a psychical apparatus packed with latent potentialities, power and possibilities; saints, prophets and Yogis are a living proof of this fact. A philosophical insight into the psychical being of man drives us into believing in the reality to the Cosmic Consciousness of the Divine Life Force as the basis, as the life of psychical entities. We need to understand man not only at his biological and mental, but at his psychical and spiritual levels.

25th August
Man: A Centre of Limitless Powers

Man has within himself tremendous powers and latent faculties of which he has really never had any conception. He must awaken these dormant powers by the practice of Yoga. As he progresses in the path, new powers, new faculties, new qualities are unfolded in him. After such an unfoldment he can change his environment, influence others, subdue the minds of others, and heal others. He can command the material wealth. He can conquer the internal and external nature, and enter into superconscious state.

26th August
The Inheritance of an Endless Empirical Past

All that you have inherited, all that you have brought with you through innumerable crores of births in the past, all that you have seen, heard, enjoyed, tasted, read or known either in this life or in the past lives are hidden in your subconscious mind. Why don't you master the technique of concentration and the way of commanding your subconscious mind and make full and free use of all that knowledge?

27th August
Man: His Divine Heritage

Courage, power, strength, wisdom and joy are your Divine Heritage from the Absolute: they are your birthright. You are centre of thought, power and influence. Never forget this. Introspect. Direct your attention towards the Knowledge of the Self.

You have a body, but you are not the body. This body is an instrument or servant of the soul, and not its prison. Know that the body is the temple of the radiant Spirit or self-effulgent Atman or Soul within, which controls and moves all the faculties of the mind and body. Know that you are breathing the breath of the Spirit, but not a physical breath.

28th August
Man: His Divine Destiny

Be men among subhuman beings, the immortals among mortals, gods among saints, and one with the Supreme Lord amongst all gods. Know yourselves and shine in your native Light. This is your glorious destiny. The poetic genius, the religious genius, the philosophic genius, are all but faint flashes of the inner Light latent in your own heart. Make ceaseless efforts, seize this inner Light and live as men who embody in themselves a Buddha and Christ.

29th August
Man: His Essential Nature

Thy essential nature is Existence Eternal. Immortality is thy very birthright. Birth and death, life here and hereafter are just fleeting phenomena, to which thou art unaffected. Witness. Thy inner Self is birthless, imperishable and permanent Existence-Knowledge-Bliss. Know this and banish all fear of death. Realise the Self and for ever soar beyond death!

30th August
The Infinite Delight: The Only Sphere
Naturally Suited to Man's Existence

A fish had accidentally jumped out of the water and was struggling. A merciful gentleman took pity and carried the fish home, put it on a warm bed, bathed it. massaged it—in fact, provided it with all the comforts he could afford. Yet, the fish was still struggling. He threw it back into the water; and it instantly began to swim happily. Man too is out of his element. The ignorant man of the world, is attached to his perishable body, mind, etc., and so suffers. But he would be ever happy again as soon as he realises his Real Nature, Satchidananda Svaroopa.

Man has forgotten his essential, divine nature. He thinks he is a separate individual. He separated himself from the Absolute on account of ignorance and egoism. So, he feels miserable.

If man kills his egoism and sense of separateness, if he annihilates desires and cravings, if he identifies himself with the Infinite, all limitations, imperfections, and miseries will end. He will attain immortality and eternal bliss.

Chapter 24
SADHAKA AND SOME ASPECTS OF SADHANA

31st August
Typical Personality-Traits of an Aspirant

The aspirant is wide awake in every part of his nature. He is ever vigilant and diligent. His presence is more eloquent than his words. His words are as unambiguous as his motives are pure. Fearless and undaunted in spirits, he has the strength of an elephant, the courage of a lion, the vigour of an oak and the purity of the Himalayan snow.

1st September
The Habit of Dilly-Dallying

Some aspirants have got the habit of wandering aimlessly. They cannot stick to one place even for a week. The wandering habit must be checked. They want to see new places, new faces and want to talk with new people. A rolling stone gathers no mass. A Sadhaka should stick to one place at least for a period of twelve years (One Tapas period). Sadhana suffers if one wanders constantly. Those who want to do rigorous Tapas or

Sadhana and study must stay in one place. Too much walking produces weakness and fatigue.

2nd September
Several Succeeding Stages of the Purificatory Process

The individual consciousness is made to pass through varying strata of mental and emotional states, pure, neutral as also impure, as the muddy water is made to pass through a tray of sand, charcoal and some germicidal medium, for the task of filtering away of gross impurities, the rough grains of the sands of worldly experiences suit and suffice admirably. But for the subtler impurities like the gaseous ones in water a medium like black charcoal is required. This is the recrudescence of disturbingly unspiritual thoughts and tendencies that dismay and upset the Sadhakas on the onward course of their spiritual development. The process takes place almost entirely upon the mental and emotional planes. Their inner working is very curious and interesting.

3rd September
The Core of Conscious Spiritual Effort

So vehement, self-assertive and rebellious is the egoistic self of man that it refuses to be changed from its vicious state to the state of virtue, goodness and saintliness. It is a great blunder to think that the mere act of renunciation is a sufficient achievement in the spiritual life. The eradication of egoism in all its aggressive forms comprises the very core of spirituality and all spiritual Sadhanas.

4th September
Necessity for a Decisive Step

Do not go on thinking of 'ifs' and 'buts'. Your environments, family history and previous mental tendencies are all, in fact conducive to quick spiritual progress. If you really wish to evolve spiritually, you should at once make a start and pursue a regular and steady course of Sadhana. Do not worry over physical and mental obstructions or unhelpful circumstances. They exist to test your sincerity and inner strength and to give you a fillip from time to time.

5th September
Retroaction of Samskaras in Sadhana

When the aspirant does intense Sadhana to obliterate the old Samskaras, they try to rebound upon him with redoubled force and vengeance. They take forms and appear before him as stumbling-blocks. The old Samskaras of hatred, enmity, jealousy, feelings of shame, respect, honour, fear, etc., assume grave forms. Samskaras are not imaginary non-entities; they turn into actualities when opportunities crop up. The aspirant should not feel discouraged; for they will lose their past momentum and force from their parting kick after sometime and die by themselves. Instead of getting alarmed at their presence, the aspirant should plunge himself in dynamic spiritual practices.

6th September
Principle and Its Perversion—I

There is the truism, i.e., "Vairagya is really a mental state, mental detachment." The mind takes hold of this definition to justify a heedless sensual life without self-restraint, or principle. The argument will always be, "O! I am not attached to all this. I can rise above it in a moment. I enjoy it as a master. Mentally I am detached." Contact with Vishayas has toppled down even Tapasvins like Visvamitra. Therefore, do not take Vairagya lightly. Cultivate Vairagya diligently. Safeguard your Vairagya carefully. Be vigilant. Watch the mind!

7th September
Principle and Its Perversion—II

The caution not to go to extremes in Tapasya also gets a similar fate. Man's normal nature is sensuous. The mind wants comforts and hates austerity. The indiscriminating aspirant conveniently ignores the qualifying adjective "extremes" in the advice quoted above and views all Tapasya with disfavour. The result is to degenerate into luxury, lose even the minimum of Titiksha and become a slave to hundred wants. The warning is against foolish extremes but to a Sadhaka in the early stages a certain degree of austerity is essential for development.

8th September
The True Import of Self-control
Self-control is a universal rule, which applies to all men and all women at all places and at all times. It is the very key to beatitude. Indulgence in objects is the effect of the failure of the individual to discriminate the Truth from untruth. Desire to have contact with and enjoy external things is the outcome of the ignorance of the Truth which is God. Self-control is the restraint of the outgoing tendencies of the mind and the senses and the centering of the same in the Truth which is the Universal One. This is Dharma which supports the life of the universe. Adharma is selfishness and egoism of nature which leads to self-imprisonment, suffering and failure in life.

9th September
Struggling Aspirant's Sheet-Anchor
Vichara, the ever-present reflection on the why and wherefore of life and things; Viveka, the ever-present discrimination between the perishable and the Imperishable, the unreal and the Real; and Vairagya, the passionate revolt from selfishness and sensuality—these three constitute the lifebelt, the wings and the eyes of every earnest seeker after Truth.

10th September
Aspirant: An Individual Apart
Vigilant among the careless, awake among the sleepers, restrained among the indulgent, reflective among the thoughtless, the wise aspirant boldly marches forward, reaches the goal now and here and attains Immortality and Eternal Bliss.

Mark the three processes that take place in the mind during meditation. These are: CONTEMPLATION, FILLING, IDENTIFICATION. Remember these three word-images. Repeat them mentally while doing Sadhana. Contemplate on the Atman. Fill the mind with Atman. Be silent. Know That.

11th September
The Hidden Enemies of the Aspirants
A beehive is all quiet; when you disturb it with a stick, bah! swarms of bees start chasing you. Our inside also is like that,

all the evils are there; but so long as they are not attacked by the rod of Sadhana they do not seem to bother us. But once they sense the impending danger, they start harassing you with all their might. Be bold and face all obstacles.

12th September
Factors That Run Counter to Progress
You should laugh in a mild, delicate and decent manner. Silly giggling, guffaw or boisterous, indecent, unrefined laughter in a rude manner should be given up, because it prevents the spiritual progress and destroys serenity of mind and serious magnanimous attitude. Sages smile through their eyes. It is grand and thrilling sight. Intelligent aspirants only can understand this. Avoid childishness and silliness.

13th September
The Rewards of Spiritual Endeavour
Sadhana gives you inner life, introspection inner vision and an unruffled state of mind under all conditions of life. You will become a changed being. You will have a new heart and a new vision too. A new thrill of spiritual current will pass through your entire being. A wave of spiritual bliss will sweep over you. There are no words to express this inner experience. Even when you get a glimpse of Truth of the Supreme Being, your whole life will be changed.

14th September
Spiritual Sadhana and Its Results
By conscious exercise of the power of the will, in the light of the knowledge acquired after a profound study of Prasthanatraya and experience, one has to throw out secret thoughts, eliminate inner hankering, overcome subtle desires, abandon selfish interests and lift the soul out of all human passions and prejudices, predilections and cross-purposes: this Sadhana engenders in the aspirant an 'emptiness' of heart, the stillness of the mind, philosophic poise and a spiritual vision.

Sadhana removes the obstacles and purifies the heart. It removes also the tossing of the mind or Vikshepa. It tears down the veil of ignorance, and then the self-luminous Reality in you shines by itself.

15th September
Sisyphean Character of Sadhana

How patiently and cautiously the fisherman watches the bait to catch a single fish! How energetically and untiringly does the student work for passing his M.Sc. Examination! How smart and careful is the surgeon in the operation theatre when the patient is on the table! How alert is the lawyer, when he is arguing the case in the session! How vigilant is the captain of a steamer when there is a cyclone or iceberg! Even so, the aspirant will have to work hard in the practice of Yoga, if he cares to realise fully the fruits of Yoga and Asamprajnata Samadhi.

Chapter 25
GUIDE AND THE SPIRITUAL GUIDANCE

16th September
The Guide: A Constitutional Necessity

The desire to seek help to search for light, to look up to higher powers, is inborn in all beings. The incapacity to achieve the ideals of the aspirations that spring from the heart, the anguish which accompanies such incapacity and the knowledge of the existence of the superior powers, obliges the individuals to take shelter under those that are endowed with the ability to lift them up to higher level. The world is a dramatic scene of dependence of beings on others that can fill up what they lack.

17th September
Greatness of the Gurus

As the human consciousness is entwined with animal instincts and drives, as man is liable to be confused and deluded by experiences of the surface-consciousness propelling the impetuous worldly will and riotous emotions, the aid of a higher power of knowledge is solicited. This power of knowledge is embodied in the Masters, the Gurus, whom the Sadhaka approaches for help. A glance, a touch, a word from them suffices to lift the soul of the aspirant; and their compassion towards the disciples is proverbial; it is unbounded, a veritable mass of love and wisdom.

18th September
Indispensability of Guidance from Guru

Cases of those, who had attained perfection without study under any Guru, should not be cited as authorities against the necessity for a Guru; for such great men are the "exceptions" in spiritual life and not the common normality. They come into existence as spiritual masters as a result of the intense service, study and meditation practised in their previous lives. They had already studied under their Gurus. Their present birth is only its continuative spiritual effort. Hence, the importance of the Guru is not lessened thereby.

19th September
Nil Desperandum

There is a lesson in everything. There is a lesson in each experience. Learn it, and become wise. Every failure is a stepping stone to success. Every difficulty or disappointment is a trial of your faith. Every unpleasant incident is a test of your trust in God. Every disease is a Karmic purgation. Every temptation is a test of your spiritual strength. Therefore, nil desperandum. March forward hero!

Forget the lapses. Don't get dejected if desires persist. Give a higher direction to the mental energies. Have a high Ideal in life.

Pay no attention to negative thoughts. Consider them as insignificant, beneath your notice.

20th September
Psychological Wisdom and Reasons for Courage

Brooding over impure thoughts adds to their evil force. Do not become a prey to these haunting dangerous thoughts. Entertain counter-thoughts: good sublime thoughts of God and His Divine Glory. By Japa, fasting, charity and selfless service, you can easily destroy the impurities of the complex mind. The evil thoughts, for lack of attention and by the pressure of good thoughts, will die a natural death. What was the state of Valmiki, Jagai, Madhai and Ajamila in the beginning? Were they not rogues of the first waters? Where is the cause for despair? Be sincere and make efforts.

21st September
The Tragedy of a Wasted Life

Be cautious, vigilant and circumspect. Reflect and meditate. People are immersed in worldliness. They have no time to think of spiritual things or the higher Power within them. The so-called cultured and educated people develop their intellects earn money, hold some rank and position, get vain and empty titles and honour and pass away. Is this not really sad? Is this not highly lamentable?

22nd September
The Childlike Heart

Your heart must be as pure as the white snow and as clear as the crystal. Just as you cannot see a clear and correct reflection in a corrugated, dust-coated mirror, even so, if your heart is cobwebbed by selfish desires and corrugated by hypocrisy and crookedness, you can hardly know the real nature of God. The spiritual aspirant must therefore cultivate a heart like that of a child.

23rd September
The Folly of Human Judgment

A dirty mirror produces a dirty image. A clear mirror gives a clear image. People with a dirty mind judge others according to their own standards of judgment and thereby commit serious blunders. If they see even a good moral man passing along the road with a woman, at once they will entertain some strong suspicion and scandalise him then and there. They have no other work besides scandal-mongering. Pitiable indeed is the lot of such people! Once a son of peasant was drinking some cold water with his mother in a lonely place during their journey to a neighbouring village. Another traveller suspected that these were immoral people and were drinking liquor. Later on, when he found out the truth, he repented very much. Therefore, be careful in your judgment of others.

Chapter 26

THE DYNAMICS OF DEVOTION
24th September
Devotion: A Fruition of Detachment and Exalted Emotional Experience

Devotion to God is not a simple emotion. It is the result of intense Vairagya and Sattvic Bhava. You should possess the good qualities extolled in the Ramayana. Otherwise, emotion may raise you temporarily to a kind of ecstasy, but you cannot experience the Divine Consciousness thereby. Devotion is a fruit which ripens gradually through the processes of self-restraint and virtue. There is no Sadhana for Bhagavat-Sakshatkara without intense Vairagya. Only after detachment from the world of things, it is possible to have the attainment of God. Do not allow the mind to think of pleasure-centres.

25th September
Services Tendered by Devotion

Devotion is the essential condition of Brahma Vidya. It is the sweetness of life that softens the heart, and removes jealousy, hatred, lust, anger, egoism, pride, arrogance. When one develops all-embracing and all-inclusive love, the petty life of hurry, worry, excitement and competition seems to him as nothing, when compared to the everlasting life of eternal sunshine and bliss in the soul within.

The path of devotion is easier than any other way of approach to God. In Vedanta and Yoga, there is the risk of a fall. In the path of devotion, there is no risk as the devotee receives full support and help from God.

26th September
The Settled Latencies of Love

Love begets love. Love does not rest content with merely loving, but flows out in acts of service. Love is blissful only when it freely gives its self. Love must be revealed in service; otherwise love has no value or love is no love. Love cheerfully sacrifices, love willingly suffers. Such a love illumines and blesses life.

Love for God or devotion is not mere emotionalism, but is the tuning of the will as well as the intellect with the Divine. It is supreme love of God. It blossoms afterwards into Jnana or Wisdom Divine. It leads to immortality or God-realisation. It is Bhakti that is the direct approach to the ideal through the heart.

27th September
The Devotee and the Cultivated Love

Love grows wildly in the ignorant man's heart. There is the luscious fruit of love in a corner of the heart; but the entire heart is strewn with thorns of hatred, jealousy and so many other vicious qualities, that the charm of love is marred. There are the bushes of lust, anger and greed, which hide within them the widest animals. Love lies hidden far beneath and far beyond reach. It is as good as non-existent. But in the case of a true devotee of the Lord, this love has been cultured, and the garden of his heart is cleared of the thorns of vicious qualities, of the bushes of lust, anger and greed. Love of God, which is the sweetest of fragrance, wafts from such a heart.

28th September
Figurative Representation of Spiritual Excellencies

In the garden of your heart plant the lily of love, the rose of purity, the Champaka of courage, the Mandara of humility and the lady-of-the-night of compassion. Cultivate a melting heart, a giving hand, kindly speech, a life of service, equal vision and an impartial attitude.

Kindle love divine in thy heart, for this is the immediate way to the Kingdom of God. Pray to the Lord. Sing His glory. Recite His Name. Become a Channel of His Grace. Seek His will. Do His Will. Surrender yourself unto the Lord. He will become your charioteer on the field of life. You will reach the destination, the abode of Immortal Bliss.

29th September
Twin Dependency of Devotion

The strength and intensity of devotion depend upon the completeness of self-surrender and sacrifice. As the vast majority of persons keep certain subtle desires for secret gratification, they do not grow in devotion. The two obstacles to self-surrender are desire and egoism.

Devotion can be practised under all conditions and by all alike. Learning, austere penance, study of Vedas, and brilliant intellect are not needed for the attainment of devotion. What is wanted is constant and living remembrance of God, coupled with faith. That is the reason why the path of Devotion is available to everyone.

30th September
Devotion: A Ritual, A Discipline, A Meditation

By fasting and observing vigil throughout the day and night on special religious occasions like Sivaratri, the aspirant, the devotee, gives himself up to the Grace of the Lord and has his body, speech and mind offered to Him. There is nothing of man left in him: he has surrendered his personality to Siva in the form of devout service. This divine worship is a ritual for the body, a discipline for speech and a meditation for the mind. With this as unfailing aids, the soul traverses beyond itself and seeks to gain ingress to the haven of peace and bliss.

The child thinks of the mother and mother alone. A passionate husband thinks of his wife and wife alone. A greedy man thinks of his money and money alone. Even so, the devotee should entertain in his heart the picture of his Ishtam and Ishtam alone. Then he can have Darshan of God easily.

Devotion transmutes man into Divinity. It intoxicates the devotee with divine love. It gives him eternal satisfaction. It makes him perfect. It weans the mind from sensual objects. It makes him rejoice in God.

Chapter 27
EVIDENCES OF THE DIVINE PRESENCE

1st October
Interrogatory Approaches to the Supreme Intelligence

The display of Intelligence is seen in every inch of creation. Can the psychologist manufacture a mind? Can the scientist explain whence the Nature's laws are? Ever since the beginning of creation some miraculous and mysterious power has, undoubtedly, been at work. You may call this "Mysterious Power", or "Father in Heaven," "Jehovah", "Allah", "Substance", "Brahman", "Ahura-Mazda". Realise this truth; all power and knowledge shall be added unto you.

2nd October
Rhetorical Questions on the Reality of God

How do you account for the ceaseless aspiration in Man for perfection, if that perfection does not exist? How can this constantly changing universe ever have any value except on the presupposition of a permanent, unchanging Substance? Why do you cry for perpetual peace in a world: which is ever-changing and dying? Is there not God who is never-dying and the never-diseased Being supporting this ever-dying and ever-diseased shallow world?

3rd October
The Intangible Power Behind the World-Show

Behind this world-show, behind these physical phenomena, behind these names and forms, behind the feelings, thoughts, emotions and sentiments, there dwells the silent witness, the immortal friend and real well-wisher, the Purusha or World-Teacher the unseen Governor, the unknown Yogi, the invisible Power, the hidden Sage. That is the only permanent Reality and the living Truth. The goal of human life is to realise the Reality behind the changing phenomena.

4th October
The Reality of the Unseen

Unseen, with faithful hands, He helps you. Unheard He hears your speech. Unknown He knows your thoughts. He is pure, all-pervading Consciousness. He is the end of all spiritual exercises and Yogic practices. Union with Him is the goal of human endeavours and life. Lasting realisation of His Concrete Presence must be the be-all and end-all of your existence.

Be firm in your belief in the guidance of God. Stick to it. Do not concern yourself with what happens around you. There may be happiness or misery. Be equally indifferent to both and abide in the faith of God.

5th October
Manifestations that Disclose Divine Wisdom

Every breath that flows through the nose, every throb of the heart, every artery that pulsates in the body, every thought that arises in the mind, speaks to you that God is here. The music of the sweet singer, the lectures of the powerful orator, the poems of the reputed poets, the inventions of the able scientists, the operations of the dexterous surgeons, the utterances of the holy saints, the thoughts of the Gita, the revelations of the Upanishads, speak of God and His Wisdom.

6th October
Nature: A Mirror of Divine Omnipotence

Every flower that wafts fragrance, every fruit that attracts you, every gentle breeze that blows, and every river that smoothly flows, speak of God and His Mercy. The vast ocean with its powerful waves, the mighty Himalayas with its glaciers, the bright sun and the shining stars in the firmament, the lofty tree with its wide branches, the cool springs in the hills and dales, sing in wordless utterance His Omnipotence.

7th October
The Finite Display of Divine Attributes

Sun brings the message that the Lord is Self-luminous; ocean reveals to you that Brahman is infinite; ether speaks to you that

Atman is all-pervading. The flower brings the message that the Lord is Beauty of beauties; Himalayas whisper in your ears about the grandeur of the Soul. Thunder brings the message that God is Omnipotent; the seed talks to you that God is the Source of everything. The Ganga murmurs to you that the Lord is ever pure.

8th October
The Meaning and Spirit of Truth

To the spiritual aspirant Truth is more than truth-speaking. Truth is God or the Absolute. It is Truth that triumphs not untruth. Truth is right, untruth is wrong; that which elevates one and takes one nearer to God is right, that which brings one down and takes one away from God is wrong. God is the indivisible unity of conscious existence. Control over passions constitutes the essence of truth. Self-denial or refraining from greedy indulgence is truth. Truth is eternal life and existence, untruth is change, decay and death. Love is truth; hatred is untruth. There is no greater sin than hatred and battle. Relative truths are valid only so long as they do not contradict absolute truth which is eternal in the highest sense.

9th October
The Benign Power

Believe in the supreme Power of God. That Supreme Power will guide you, strengthen you and comfort you. You will be peaceful in the midst of trials, adversities, defeats and tempestuous life. God is the unseen Teacher who through his great sons, through nature herself teaches men the secret and source of the attainment of eternal bliss.

The Lord is within you, He is seated in your heart. Whatever you see, hear, taste and touch is God. Therefore hate not anybody, cheat not anybody, harm not anybody. Love all and be one with all. You will soon attain eternal bliss, immortality, and perennial joy.

10th October
The All-Pervasive Lord

The Petromax does not talk, but it shines and sheds light all around. The jasmine does not speak, but it wafts its fragrance everywhere. The lighthouse sounds no drum, but sends its friendly-light to the mariner. The Unseen beats no gong, but Its omnipresence is felt by the dispassionate and discriminating sage.

You want laboratory proofs? Very fine, indeed! You wish to limit the illimitable, all-pervading God in your test tube, blowpipe land chemicals. God is the source for your chemicals. He is the substratum for your atoms, electrons and molecules. Without Him, no atom or electron will move. He is the Inner Power and Ruler.

11th October
The Being Is Beyond the Mind

To define God is to deny God. You can define a finite object only. How can you define the limitless Being? If you define God you are limiting the limitless one, you are confining Him within the concepts of the mind. God is beyond the reach of gross mind, but He can be realised through meditation with the help of a pure, subtle and one-pointed mind.

You cannot find God by the intellect. But you can find Him by feeling, meditation, experience, and realisation. Though you do not see the stars in the daytime, yet they do exist. Even so, though you cannot see God with these physical eyes, yet He does exist. If you gain intuition, you will behold Him.

12th October
Amazing Response of the All-Merciful

If the aspirant takes one step nearer to the Divine Being, it will come in a hundred leaps and bounds nearer to him. Such is the nature of the Eternal Being. For every bit of action that is done for Its sake, you receive is millionfold in return! This fact is beautifully illustrated in the workings of Bhagavan Sri Krishna for the good of His devotees.

13th October
The Laws and Love of God

God loves you even when you turn away from Him. How much more shall He love you, if you turn to Him again with faith and devotion! Very great is His love, greater than the greatest Himalayas, deeper than the deepest ocean.

The laws of God are in your breath, blood, and eyes; in the outer world, they are in the air, water, earth and planets. Listen to the words of God in the flowing breath; tune yourself to the rhythm of the pulse—beats and heart throbs. A life lived in accordance with the Laws of God is indeed the blessed life of greatness and universality.

14th October
The Thought of the Divine

Even if you think of the Lord or of Lord Vishnu or Siva, only once, even if for once you form a mental image of these all-pervading, omniscient deities, the Sattvic material of the mind will increase a bit. If you think of them crores of times, your mind will be filled with a large quantity of Sattva. Constant thinking of God thins out the mind and destroys the Vasanas and Sankalpas. Realise the great importance and value of thinking of the Divine.

You have the urge of hunger. There is food to appease the hunger. You have the urge of thirst. There is water to quench the thirst. There is the urge to be always happy. There must be something to satisfy this urge. This something is God, an embodiment of happiness. God, Perfection, Joy, are synonymous terms.

Chapter 28

FATE, FATALISM AND FREE-WILL

15th October
The Mechanism of Destiny

Every act produces in the performer a double effect, one in the inner nature in the form of a tendency, good or bad, and the other in the form of fruit, reward or punishment. The past Karma influences the present life in two ways, first in the form of character or tendency internally and as fate externally. If you do an action, it creates a Samskara or subtle impression in the subconscious mind or Chitta. Samskara causes a tendency. Tendency develops into a habit by repetition of the actions. The habit manifests as character. Character develops into destiny. This is the order: Samskara, tendency, habit, character and destiny.

16th October
Free Will and Fatalism

Vasishtha asks Rama to do Purushartha. Do not yield to fatalism. It will induce inertia and laziness. Purushartha is right exertion. Prarabdha is Purushartha of last birth. You sow an action and reap a habit; a habit sown results in character. You sow a character and reap a destiny. Man is the master of his destiny. You yourself make your destiny. You can undo it if you like. All faculties, energies and powers are latent in you. Unfold them and become free.

There is a certain definite connection between what is being now done by you and what will happen to you in the future. Sow always the seeds which will bring pleasant fruits and which will make you happy herein and hereafter.

17th October
Fate: Energies of the Hidden Past Working in the Present

Hard fate is the name given to that unseen force which brings unpleasant experiences and tests one's patience, and in which the man concerned is inclined to believe that he deserved much better fate than he obtained. There is no such thing as accident or chance or fate or luck in life excepting the results of one's own previous actions which have all these appellations.

Every thought, desire, imagination, sentiment causes reaction. Virtue brings its own reward; vice brings its own punishment. This is the working of the law of reaction. God neither punishes the wicked nor rewards the virtuous. It is their own Karmas that bring reward and punishment.

18th October
The Boomerang Character of All Action

Any action is bound to react upon one with equal force and effect. If you do some good to another man, you are really helping yourself; because, there is nothing else besides the one all-pervading Self and Power. Your virtuous actions will react upon you with good effects. They bring you joy and happiness. Your wrong, unjust actions will react upon you with bad, miserable effects. They will bring you sorrow, grief and affliction. Therefore, always live to do good to others. Be kind to all. Never hurt others.

19th October
Construct a Wheel of Fortune

Entertain holy desires. You will shine in Divine Glory. Under the security of the changeless law of cause and effect, a man can serenely proceed to achieve anything he desires to accomplish. Therefore entertain Divine thoughts. You are sure to succeed in your well directed efforts. In nature nothing is lost.

People of gigantic will have developed their will through Karma done in countless births. The potencies of these actions collect together and in one birth the struggling man bursts out as a giant like Buddha, Jesus and Sankara. Patient, indefatigable effort is needed.

20th October
Fatalism and the Doctrine of Karma

Belief in Karma is diametrically opposed to the doctrine of fatalism. Fatalism causes inertia, lethargy and weakness of will and bondage. It annihilates faith, induces terrible fear in the people, destroys ethics, checks growth and evolution, whereas the doctrine of Karma is an incentive to action to better one's condition. It is a source of solace and peace. It gives opportunities for growth and evolution. It gives a positive, definite word of assurance that, although the present, of which man himself is the creator or the author, is unalterable or irrevocable, he may better his future by changing his thoughts, habits, tendencies and mode of action. Even a forlorn and helpless man is made cheerful when he understands this doctrine of Karma. It affords the most rational explanation of fate.

Chapter 29

FROWNS OF FORTUNE AND SPIRITUAL GROWTH

21st October
Progress by Ordeal

The devotee has to pass through fiery ordeals. Prahlada had to jump in the fire. Harischandra had to sell his queen and become the slave of a sweeper. King Sibi offered his own flesh. Therefore, be prepared to pass the ordeals. Spiritual path is not a rosy one. The path is easy for one who is wise and vigilant, firm in his resolves, and has an undying aspiration to attain the highest peak of Truth.

If God gives trials, He gives also new strength to bear the trials. There is no room for worry. Say, "Thy Will be done." You will grow quickly.

22nd October
Conditions for Sainthood

Difficulties come and go. They strengthen your will and make the mind move more and more towards God. Saints and supermen have been moulded out of difficulties and adversities. Pray, His Grace will smoothen the path and give strength.

Life is a series of conquests. Man evolves, grows, expands, gains various experiences through struggle. If you want to continue your existence and progress on the path, difficulties and struggle are essential. You cease to exist and make progress, the moment you cease to struggle. Self-realisation and sainthood demand very great struggle.

23rd October
Pruning Process of Suffering and Pain

Suffering is a necessary element in the spiritual growth or evolution of the soul. It produces the spirit of dispassion or Vairagya, develops the power of endurance and will-force; it turns the mind more and more towards God. Pain has a purifying and perfecting power. It corrects and disciplines man; it softens the hardness of his heart, subdues his pride, and helps him to develop fortitude, patience, strength of soul and mercy.

The nearer a devotee approaches the Lord, the greater are the trials. They come merely to strengthen his power of endurance and exhaust his Prarabdha Karma. Greet them with good cheer. Keep your inner peace, in all conditions. This is Yoga.

24th October
Necessity of Adversity

Adversity has the power of eliciting talents, capacities which in prosperous circumstances have remained dormant. It draws out the faculties of the wise, makes the idle industrious. A smooth ocean never made one a dexterous Captain of a ship. The storms of adversity rouse the faculties and talents of an individual and generate prudence, skill, fortitude, courage, patience, and perseverance. Adversity makes one think, invent and discover. Great persons and saints have been tried, smelted, polished and glorified through the furnace of adversity.

25th October
Results of Trials

Trial is a crucible into which nature throws a man whenever she wants to mould him into a sublime Superman. There can be no strength, no success, without suffering. Every suffering is meant for one's upliftment and development. It augments the power of endurance, mercy, faith in God and removes egoism. Understand this and develop inner strength.

All trials and difficulties are temporary. They will pass away. Have faith. Fear not. Worry not. Be cheerful. Contact God by regular Japa, Kirtan and study of holy books.

26th October
Sequences of Dispensation

Man applauds, commends and expresses gratitude for the creation and preservation parts of the Divine plan, but when its logical sequence in the form of destruction is made manifest, he frantically and frenziedly entreats the intervention and aid of the Lord, as though this destructive process is being wrought by some third agency distinct and different from the Supreme One. Man must behold and gaze at Truth square in the face. The realm of justice has no place for the play of emotion.

27th October
The Right Frame of Mind

Never condemn yourself. Never lose faith in yourself. Seek to know Thyself. Cheer yourself and regain confidence. Assert and realise that you are a child of God and that all the wealth of the Divine is yours. Shut your mind against these traitors: fear, disease, worry and in their stead, invite confidence, courage, peace, health. If only you know the unlimited power that is within you, there is no undertaking in which you cannot succeed. The progress you would achieve will be amazing. Scatter joy and you will harvest it. Distribute wealth and you will have abundance. Radiate happiness and you will reap it.

If the wick within the lamp is very small, the light also will be small. If the wick is very big, the light also will be powerful. Similarly, if a man is pure, if he practises meditation, the manifestation or expression of his Self will be powerful. He will radiate a big light. If he is unregenerate and impure, he will be like a burntup charcoal. The greater the wick, the greater the light. Likewise, the purer the soul, the greater the expression.

Chapter 30
CONTINENCE AND THE TECHNIQUES OF SEX-SUBLIMATION

28th October
The Transformation of the Seminal Energy

With the shrewdest common sense and the deepest wisdom, the Yogi investigator has been that repression and forced abstinence is not the rational method. That has not been his aim; he has been thorough in his research into the subject. He has successfully perfected a method of transforming the gross seminal energy into a refined subtle force through a process of sex-sublimation. Through a marvellous system of Asanas, Mudras and

Bandhas expounded in the science of Hatha Yoga, the sex-energy is controlled, conserved, and converted.

The vital energy, Veerya, which supports your life, which shines in your sparkling eyes, which beams in your shining cheeks, is a great treasure for you. It is the quintessence of blood. Convert it into spiritual Power.

29th October
The Maintenance of Brahmacharya

Even looking at a person of the opposite sex is forbidden, for the creative activity of the psychological organ will at once manifest itself and start the diversifying function. No kind of contact with the opposite sex is allowed. Even a sexual thought has the baneful effect of irritating the formative power. The restraint of the action of the creative psyche is immediately loosened the moment it is invaded by the thought of the working of the opposite sex. Thus the spiritual energy gets disintegrated and does not serve the purpose of constructive Realisation. Objects which rouse the lower appetite are to be dispensed with and company of persons in whom there is sexual preponderance should be avoided.

30th October
Spiritual Psychology of Self-Attraction

Sex-attraction, sexual thoughts, sexual urge are the three great obstacles on the path of God-realisation. Even if the sexual urge vanishes, the sex-attraction remains for a long time and troubles the aspirants. The organ of sight does great mischief. Destroy the lustful look, the adultery of the eye. Try to see the Divine Lord in all faces. Again and again generate the currents of dispassion, discrimination and spiritual enquiry.

Lack of spiritual Sadhana is the main cause for all sexual attractions. Mere theoretical abstention from sensuality will not bring you good results. You must mercilessly cut off all formalities in social life and lead a pious life. Leniency to internal lower tendencies will land you in the region of suffering.

31st October
Sixfold Method of Sex-Sublimation
No spiritual progress is possible without the practice of celibacy. As the semen is a dynamic force, it should be converted into Ojas or spiritual energy by the sixfold method for sex-sublimation: (1) by pure and sublime thoughts. (2) by repetition of the Names of the Lord, (3) by prayer and worship, (4) by meditation, (5) by spiritual feelings, and (6) by the practice of Pranayama. Thus sex-energy should be transmuted into the Ojas Sakti and stored in the brain. It can be utilised for divine contemplation and spiritual pursuits. A man who has great deal of Ojas in his brain can turn out immense mental work, is very intelligent, has a magnetic aura around his face and possesses a rare lustre in his eyes. His is an awe-inspiring personality.

1st November
Philosophy and Forms of Physical Passion
The moment there is a lustful craving for any sexual person there is a psychological perpetration of adultery. The astral body operates in thinking. Further Brahmacharya is defined as not merely restraint of the forces of self-reproduction but also of self-preservation. Gluttony, arrogance, anger, greed or miserliness, audacity, jealousy, infatuation and such material tendencies are a fall from Brahmacharya and a failure of the endeavour to attain spiritual perfection. Anger is the product of passion; excessive sleep and inertia form the negative phases of cupidity. Talkativeness is a misuse of constructive energy and is a break of Brahmacharya. Brahmacharya is a fasting of the objective tendencies of the mind and a directing inward of the same to help in Self-Illumination.

2nd November
Sublimation of the Emotion of Anger
Anger and muscular energy can also be transmuted into Ojas. Should the wave of anger possess you, repair to a quiet room and have a good loud hearty laugh and make it effervesce into a pure upsurge of good cheer and laughter. Or sit still and send out wave after wave of love, of blessing and goodwill, to the entire universe, from the bottom of your heart. Repeat again and again the sublime verses of Santi-patha of the Upanishads.

You will be filled with overflowing cosmic love. All anger-Vasanas will vanish in toto, leaving in their stead a continuous thrill of motiveless love. This feeling is indeed indescribable. This Sadhana will give you a positive asset of Sattva and Prem. You will find yourself a tangibly different being after even a single genuine attempt at this process of deliberate conversion.

3rd November
An Objective Process of Sublimation

When a fit of social nature assails the aspirant, he should not allow himself to be driven out into the bazaar for gossiping or into nearest reading-room, teashop or tablechat. Go he should among the poor and the afflicted instead, and see if he can serve them in any way. He should go to the road or highway among the pilgrims and the wayfarers and seek to relieve them of their loads and lessen their burdens with pleasant and elevating conversation. Thus in the very process of giving enrich himself.

Seminal energy is a potent Sakti. A Brahmachari who has practised unbroken celibacy for full twelve years will attain the Nirvikalpa state, the moment he hears the Mahavakya—Tat Tvam Asi, Thou art That. His mind becomes extremely pure, strong and one-pointed.

4th November
An Analogy From the Field of Electrons

Even among electrons there are bachelor electrons and married electrons. Married electrons manifest in pairs. Bachelor electrons exist singly. It is these bachelor electrons only that create magnetic electric force. The power of Brahmacharya is seen even in electrons.

There are four processes in the practice of Brahmacharya. First control the sex-impulses. Then practise conservation of sex-energy. Shut out all holes through which energy leaks. Then, divert the conserved energy into the proper spiritual channels through Japa, Kirtan, selfless service, Pranayama, study, self-analysis, discrimination. Then convert or sublimate the sex-energy into Ojas or Brahma-tejas, divine energy and brilliance, by meditation on the Divine.

5th November
Restrainment of the Instinctive Practice and Its Results

Those who have discriminatively grasped the spiritual character of human life refrain from the instinctive practice of self-multiplication and devote themselves to the glorious task of directing the potential energy to conscious contemplation on the Spiritual Ideal through the triple transformation of the active, emotional and intellectual aspects of the general human nature. Such integrated persons possess a mighty power of understanding, analysis and meditation. Such Brahmacharins glow with a lustrous spiritual strength which handles with ease even the most formidable of the diversifying forces of nature. Fear is unknown to them and their divinised energy is centred on the Self, to be utilised in transcending the realm of the ego-sense. They have learnt to expand their formative power into the plenitude of the limitless life.

The practice of celibacy is not attended with any danger or disease, or undesirable results such as the various sorts of 'complex' wrongly attributed by the Western psychologists. They have a wrong and ill-founded knowledge that the ungratified sex-energy assumes the various forms of 'complex' such as touch-phobia. It is a morbid state of mind due to excessive jealousy, anger, worry, and depression brought about by various causes. On the contrary, even a little of self-restraint or a little practice of continence is an ideal 'pick-me-up'. It gives inner strength and peace of mind, invigorates the mind and nerves, helps to conserve physical and mental energy, augments memory, will-force and brain-power. It renovates the constitution, rebuilds the cells and tissues, energises digestion, and gives power to face the difficulties in the daily battle of life.

Chapter 31
PHILOSOPHY AND PHILOSOPHISING

6th November
The Pursuit of Philosophy

Habitual study of abstract problems will result in a well-developed power for abstract thinking, while flippant, hasty thinking, flying at a tangent, jumping from one point to another, will produce a restless ill-regulated mind. Study of philosophical works, right thinking, exercise of good and noble emotions, prayers and beneficent endeavours, and above all, regular and strenuous meditation are the means to improve the mind. These activities bring about a rapid growth and evolution of the mental consciousness. Take down notes when you study a book on Yoga or philosophy. This will help you in remembering the fundamental ideas. This itself is a kind of lower Samadhi, as the mind is deeply occupied in Sattvic ideas. It will check the outgoing tendencies of the mind. The mind will move towards the inner Self.

7th November

Philosophy: An Intellectual Science and an Art of Life

Philosophy is the rational aspect of religion. It is an integral part of religion in India. It is a rational enquiry into the nature of Truth. It gives clear solution for profound, subtle problems of life. It shows the way to get rid of pain and death and attain immortality and eternal bliss.

Real philosophy is a moral and intellectual science which tries to explain the reality behind appearances. It is the methodical work of the intellect which aims at the knowledge and realisation of what "really is". Philosophy can also be explained as the art of perfect life, the way not simply of explaining what ought to be, but of directly experiencing that which eternally exists.

8th November

Requisites for Philosophising

Hard thinking, persistent thinking, clear thinking, thinking to the very roots of all problems, grappling with the fundamentals of all intellectual situations, a firm grasp of and penetration into the very presuppositions of all thought and experience, is the essence of Vedantic Sadhana. Deep thinking necessitates a taking of recourse to intense Sadhana. A subtle, calm, clear pure, sharp, one-pointed intelligence is needed for understanding and meditating on the goal of the boldest of all philosophical efforts: Brahman.

9th November
A Method of Philosophising

When the aspirant sees the tempting and alluring form of a beautiful lady or a fascinating flower or any attractive form he should philosophise thus: "This beautiful lady with lustrous eyes and rosy cheeks and scarlet lips, though very tempting now, is after all a mass of flesh, fat and bones. It is nothing more than a combination of bones, nerves, skin and hair, and therefore, subject to decay. This beautiful flower will fade away in a few hours. It will turn to dust ere long. The beauty in the feminine form, in the fine flower is but a reflection of that Beauty of Beauties, the unchanging. never-dying Self within, the immortal glory of glories. May that all-pervading Presence of the All-Beautiful Lord, the source of all life, thought, consciousness and beauties, be the sole object of my love and adoration."

10th November
Some Philosophical Reflections

Friends! Is there not a higher mission in life besides eating, sleeping and talking? Is there not any higher form of (Eternal) Bliss than these transitory and illusory pleasures? Is there not a more dignified life than the sensual life? How uncertain is life here! How insecure is our existence on this earth-plane with various kinds of fear! How painful is this mundane life? Should we not attempt diligently now to reach a place where there is eternal sunshine, absolute security, perfect peace? Should we not love the Lord, pursue Truth and live the Divine Life?

11th November
The Object of Philosophic Search

Know what you seek, and then seek. What you pursue here fails to give you what you truly seek, and recedes like a mirage. Nothing on earth can give you everlasting happiness. Youth fades like the evening flowers, strength vanishes like the rent cloud; the beauty of the body quickly gives way to the ugly death. Your pleasure-centres mock at you, for you have mistaken pain for happiness, mirage for water! The real object that you seek, the one treasure without which you are restless is the realisation of the imperishable bliss of Godhead within.

12th November
Science, Philosophy, Religion and the Voice of Spiritual Experience

The business of science is generalisation of phenomena; it is the function of philosophy and Yoga to explain it. Religion is the practical aspect of philosophy; philosophy is the rational aspect of religion. The scientist tries to answer the "How" of the problem; the philosopher and the Yogi, the "Why" of it. It is a mistake to say that such and such an event occurs because of certain laws of Nature. The laws of nature do not give any real explanation of phenomena. It is simply a scientist's statement in terms as general as possible of what happens under given circumstances in his expression of an observed order or uniformity in a natural phenomena. Science differs radically in its outlook from philosophical musings. Science shows a marvellous harmony of Nature; but it is the problem of philosophy and Yoga to solve the "Why" of the Nature's harmony.

Only to a spiritually blind man, the world seems to be different from God and also from himself, and it seems to him that he himself is different from God. The moment the screen from his eyes is lifted, it will be seen that what really is, is an ocean of pure consciousness, the boundless Absolute where the world and the individual are no more separate beings, but are united in its indivisible glory of Infinity and Immortality. This is the grand destination of life, the purpose of everyone's existence, the goal of all aspirations and endeavours. Brahman alone is real all else has no reality independent of Brahman.

Chapter 32
INTEGRAL YOGA AND THE LIMITATIONS OF SCIENCE

13th November
Scientific Knowledge and Yogic Experience

Science is partially unified knowledge. A scientist observes the laws of Nature, experiments in his laboratory, investigates, infers and draws exact conclusions from his observations. He understands the outward surface and the physical aspects of

Nature and knows nothing of the origin, the occult intentions and destiny of Nature. The scientist does not know as to what made and bestowed upon the ultimate particles of matter their marvellous power of varied interaction. On the contrary, the Yogi gets inner divine realisation, sees with his Yogic vision the subtle rudiments of matter, has an intimate experience of the Supreme Power and Being behind all Nature. He gets control over the five elements, clearly understands the whole mystery of creation through direct intutional knowledge.

14th November
Science and Yogic Perception

Science perceives things as they appear to normal human perception, i.e., as they appear to be whereas the Yogi perceives them as they actually are. The Yogi perceives things intuitively and knows them in their essential state. While each theory, each discovery of science, that is put forward one day is contradicted and falsified by a fresh one, the next, the realisations arrived at through Yoga are infallible, as they are the direct perceptions with the highest instrument, namely, the purified mind attuned to the Infinite.

15th November
The Limitations of Science

Scientists have not understood the whole code of Nature's laws. They have no knowledge of occult side of things of the astral, and higher planes such as Brahmaloka. The unseen world is of far greater importance than the sense-universe which is visible to the naked eye. A fully developed Yogi can function in all the planes and so he has full knowledge of the manifested Nature. Scientists have no knowledge of the subtle rudiments of matter. Life will become fuller and richer, when one develops the inner eyesight by the practice of Yoga. The knowledge of the scientists is only fragmentary or partial, whereas the knowledge of the Yogi is full and perfect.

16th November
No Oriental Magic But a System of Self-development

The supraphysical phenomena occurring in the practice of Yoga and the practitioner's experience on subtler planes are viewed with suspicion and regarded as mere oriental magic. Yoga is neither fanciful nor does it contain anything abnormal. It aims at the integral development of all faculties in man. It is the time-tested, rational way to a fuller and more blessed life that will naturally be followed by one and all in the world of tomorrow. The eminently practical nature of Yoga renders it the rational bridge between the idealism of pure philosophy and the hard realism of earthly life. It is concerned with Transcendental Life, yet it asks you to take nothing for granted. You are to follow definite methods, arrive at tangible results and experience them in your own life.

17th November
Groundwork of Yoga-Practice

All methods of Yoga have ethical training and moral perfection as their basis. The eradication of vices and the development of certain virtues form the first step in the ladder of Yoga. The disciplining of your nature and the formation of a steady and pure character through a set of right habits and regular daily observances is the next step. Upon this firm foundation of a well-established and virtuous moral character is built the further structure of Yoga.

Upon the basis of moral purity, awaken yourself to the conscious realisation of your oneness with the Supreme Self. Think of the Self continuously. As Tennyson says: "Let thy voice rise like a fountain for Me night and day." This is the real spiritual practice or Brahma-Abhyasa. It will lead you to Self-realisation.

18th November
Component Parts of Yoga-Practice

By practising Yama and Niyama, the Yogic student purifies his mind. By practising Asana, he gets steadiness and firmness of body. By practising Pranayama, he removes the tossing of mind and destroys Rajas and Tamas. By practising Pratyahara he gets mental strength, peace of mind and inner life. By the practice of Dharana he gets Ekagrata of mind. By practising Dhyana, he fills the mind with divine thoughts. By practising Samadhi, he destroys the seeds of births and deaths, and gets immortality and Kaivalya, the final beatitude, the highest end of human life.

19th November
The Pivotal Point of All Yoga

Careful reflection will show that the entire universe is in reality the projection of the human mind Manomatram Jagat. Purification and control of the mind is the central aim of all Yoga. Mind in itself is but a record of impressions that keep expressing themselves ceaselessly as impulses and thoughts. The mind is what it does. Thought impels you to action; activity creates fresh impressions in the mind-stuff. Yoga strikes at the very root of this vicious circle by a method of effectively inhibiting the functions of the mind. Yoga checks, controls and stops the root function of the mind, i.e., thought. When thought is transcended, intuition functions and Self-knowledge supervenes.

20th November
An Affirmation of Spiritual Positivism

Logical chopping, clever hair-splitting arguments, intellectual gymnastics and word-jugglery will not help you in attaining Self-realisation. You must harmoniously develop your head, heart and hand through the practice of the Yoga of Synthesis. Only then will you attain perfection and integral development.

The four Yogas are interdependent and inseparable. Service purifies and expands the heart. Love unifies. Without service and love you cannot dream of attaining Advaitic realisation of Oneness. Love is involved in service; service is love in expression. Knowledge is diffused love and love is concentrated Knowledge.

21st November
The Integration of Yogas

Have you seen the picture of Lord Siva's family? Mother Parvati is in the centre. She has Ganesha and Subrahmanya on Her sides. Ganesha is the Lord of Wisdom, Subrahmanya is the Lord of Action. Mother Parvati is an embodiment of Love. You should learn a spiritual lesson from this picture. This picture teaches that you can attain Perfection only by the practice of the Yoga of Synthesis.

Human mind has three defects—Mala or impurity, Vikshepa or tossing, Avarana or veil. Karma Yoga removes the impurity; Upasana or worship removes the tossing; Jnana Yoga tears down the veil. Only then is Self-realisation possible.

22nd November
The True Synthesis of Yoga

Our religion must educate and develop the whole man, his heart, head and hand. One-sided development is never commendable. Karma Yoga purifies and develops the hand. Bhakti Yoga destroys Vikshepa and develops the heart. Raja Yoga steadies the mind and makes it one-pointed. Jnana Yoga removes the veil of ignorance and develops will and reason. Therefore, one should practise the four Yogas. Taking Jnana Yoga as the central basis, the Sadhaka can practise the other Yogas as auxiliaries to bring in rapid progress on the spiritual path.

23rd November
Facets of Development

Action, emotion and intelligence are the three horses that are linked to this body-chariot. They should work in perfect harmony or union. Only then the chariot will run smoothly. Vedanta without devotion is quite dry. Bhakti without Jnana is not perfect. There must be integral development. You must have the head of Sankara, the heart of Buddha and the hand of Janaka.

The Yoga of Synthesis alone will develop the head, heart and hand, and lead one to perfection. To behold the one Self in all beings is Jnana, wisdom; to love the Self is Bhakti, devotion; to serve the Self is Karma, action. When the Jnana Yogi attains wisdom, he is endowed with devotion and selfless activity.

24th November
Spontaneous Ascent of Kundalini

Generally there is no genuine spiritual awakening in students. There is mere curiosity for getting some psychic or Yogic powers. That student is far from God as long as he retains some hidden desire for Siddhis. Strictly observe the ethical rules.

Transform the worldly nature first. If you become absolutely desireless, if the mental Vrittis are destroyed in toto, Kundalini will ascend by itself, without effort, through the force of purity. Remove the dross of mind. You will yourself get help and answer from within.

25th November
The Uniqueness of Asanalogy

The practice of Asanas controls the emotions, produces mental peace, distributes Prana evenly throughout the body and its different systems, helps in maintaining a healthy functioning of the internal organs and gives internal massage to the various abdominal organs. Physical exercise draws the Prana (energy) out but the Asanas send the Prana in. The practice of Asanas cures many diseases and awakens Kundalini Sakti. These are the chief advantages in the Yogic system of exercises which no other system has.

26th November
Mastery Over Nature's Powers Through Pranayama

The human body is the copy of the cosmic structure in miniature and Prana enlivens and animates the organism. Each element has gone into its constitution. The key-force behind all forces of nature is Prana. Prana is the manifest essence of all the forces that exist. The cerebrospinal system forms man's subtle switchboard. The different subtle psychic centres dominate particular elements of forces in nature. By gaining mastery over the vital astral centres located therein, man obtains control over every force of nature.

If you can control Prana, you can control all the forces of the universe, physical and mental. A Yogi can also control the omnipresent Manifesting Power from which originate all energies like magnetism, electricity, nerve-currents, vital forces, thought-vibrations, etc.

27th November
The Carnegie Principle and Raja Yoga

"Win friends and influence people": this Dale Carnegie principle is but a leaf out of the ancient Indian volume on psycho-spiritual science. Practise Yoga; the entire world will worship you.

You will unconsciously attract to yourself every living being; even gods will be at you, beck and call. Even among wild beasts and blonde brutes you will "win friends". Serve all; love all. Unfold your inner powers, through the practice of Raja Yoga.

Remember God. Turn towards God. Meditate on God. Dwell in God. See God in all. Repeat the Name of God. Realise God, here and now. You will be adored by all humanity, for centuries to come, even as Jesus and Buddha are being adored.

28th November
Uses of Yoga

Through the practice of Yoga, you can. overcome all difficulties and can eradicate all weaknesses. Through the practice of Yoga pain can be transmuted into bliss, death into immortality, sorrow into joy, failure into success and sickness into perfect health. Therefore, practise Yoga diligently.

Through Yogic discipline, mind, body and the organ of speech work together harmoniously. You can have calmness of mind at all times by practice of Yoga. You can have restful sleep. You can have increased energy, vitality, longevity, and a high standard of health. The Yoga way of life deepens your understanding and enables you to know God.

29th November
Personality of a Yogi

A growing Yogi or an aspirant who meditates regularly has a magnetic and charming personality. Those who come in contact with him are much influenced by his sweet voice, powerful speech, lustrous eyes, brilliant complexion, strong healthy body, good behaviour, virtuous qualities and Divine Nature. People derive joy, peace and strength from him. They are inspired by his speech and get elevation of mind by mere contact with him.

If the magnet is more powerful, it will influence the iron filings even when they are placed at a long distance. Even so, if the Yogi is an advanced person, he will have greater influence over the persons with whom he comes in contact. He can exert his influence on persons even when they are thousands of miles away.

30th November
Transmission of Help Through Supernormal Agencies
Through their spiritual vibrations and magnetic aura the unknown real Yogis help the world more than the "Yogis" of the platform. Preaching from the pulpits and platforms belongs to men of second grade spirituality, who have no knowledge and never put to use the supernormal faculties and powers latent in them. Great adepts and Mahatmas transmit their message through telepathy to deserving aspirants in different corners of the world. Means of communication that are supernormal to us are quite normal to a Yogi.

1st December
Most Prominent of the Methods
The ancient sages had formulated certain well-defined and workable methods by which man can establish union with the Divine. It is a means of compressing one's evolution within a single lifetime, even within a few years of this particular life. Of the many methods that are widely accepted and followed, the path of Dhyana is the highly scientific, practical, graduated system of Maharshi Patanjali, otherwise known as Ashtanga Yoga. The reason for this unique importance is that Patanjali Maharshi's system is based upon the most rationally comprehensive consideration of man in every aspect of his being. It has taken man as he is constituted fundamentally, divested of incidental association. It takes man as a centre of pure consciousness, localised within enfolding sheaths of matter of varying degrees of subtlety. Conceived in this light, man is basically the same the world over in all periods of time. This system is the universal one and is for all times, and offers a process that is practicable to every type of the average individual. It is characterised by the most intelligent synthesis and a very beautiful graduation.

2nd December
Numberless Methods of Approach
The Absolute can be conceived of in manifold forms, and manifold are the methods of approach to it in accordance with the nature of man's mind-stuff. Every cogitating creature has in fact its own religion based on a firm background of thought which

men call 'philosophy'. Philosophy is theoretical religion of the stuff of spiritual practice. It declares that beings, in spite of themselves, are urged by the truth of indivisible existence to find themselves in Its centre of experience. The human aspiration culminates in the blissful possession of eternal life; nothing short of it.

Yoga embraces in itself several methods of realising God, of approaching and experiencing the Absolute. Yoga is the science of divine living; it has nothing to do with any religious belief, traditional faith, colour, vocation or clime. Yoga is neither Eastern nor Western; it is of the world, of humanity in general. In any walk of life, at any stage and step, one can be a Yogi; Yoga admits of degrees. To become wider and deeper, more inclusive in one's being and consciousness, is the aim of Yoga; to make man one with Godhead is the goal of Yoga. Take for practice anyone of the several methods Yoga offers you and realise God here and now.

Chapter 33

VEDANTA: ITS DISCIPLINES AND ITS VALUE

3rd December
The Functions of Vedanta

Vedanta illumines, ennobles, elevates and enlightens us with its great formula, Tat Tvam Asi. It imparts to us the message that in the law of our being that Supreme Being pervades all this that is. The constituting essence and substance of our inmost being, is the one Divine Reality that is at once immanent and transcendent. A feeling of oneness with every form of life, a sense of the unity of all existence, a desire to release the best of our energies in the dynamic service of others, can arise only from a firm grasp of the essential spiritual nature of ourselves and of those around us.

4th December
Meaning of "Being Oneself"

The path of Vedanta is the most natural. It is nothing but manifesting what you exactly are in essence. Be thyself. Thou art the resplendent Atman. Be rooted in this Supreme Consciousness. Eternity is thy very nature. Realise this now and here. Deep as the ocean is thy life. Nothing can harm you. Thou art the all-pervading, immortal soul.

5th December
The Witness: A Philosophical Explanation
The Atman is called the witness, not in truth, but from the individual's standpoint of phenomenal experience in the plane of ignorance or Avidya. When the Atman is realised, there is no witnessing of another thing. This being a witness is only the individual's conception of the Atman. It does not mean that there is something different from Atman. The personal relative self involves the idea of individuality but the Absolute Atman does not involve subject-object-distinction.

The inmost self in you is the Witness; it is the Infinite Reality. It is of the nature of Satchidananda. You are That. Realise this and be free.

6th December
The Perception of the One Self
When you see any person or object, think and feel that he or it is Atman or Narayana. By incessant practice of this, Namarupa (name and form), will vanish, Atman or Narayana will shine. The world-idea will disappear. This practice demands strenuous and protracted efforts. During the course of the practice, your old Samskaras will trouble you. Boldly, you must fight against them. This spiritual practice of Samyag Jnana, will give you Samyag Darshan of Atman. You will transmute all objects into Atman. Think and feel that all actions are Atmapuja. The idea of inferiority and the idea of menial service will disappear as you see Narayana or Atman everywhere.

7th December
Principles of Vedantic Sadhana
Rise above desires. Abandon the beggarly attitude of the mind. Feel the majesty of yourself. Identify yourself with the glorious all-full self-contained Brahman. Then all desires die a natural death; they will be fulfilled. This is the secret of the fulfilment of all desires. Then, Nature will obey you and you can command

the elements, All the eight Siddhis and the nine Riddhis will roll under your feet. This is the sublime teaching of the Vedanta.

Behold the one homogeneous Self in all. Mentally repeat the formula or Mantra "OM Ek Sat-chit-ananda Atma"—'There is but one Infinite Existence-Knowledge- Delight'—whenever you perceive any form. Negate the illusory name and form and try to identify yourself with the underlying immortal Essence.

8th December
Vedantic Technique of Self-Transcendence

When emotions and impulses trouble you much, be indifferent (Udasina). Say to yourself: "Who am I?" Feel: "I am not this mind. I am the Atman, the all-pervading Spirit, Suddha Sat-Chit-Ananda. How can emotions affect me? I am Nirlipta, unattached; I am Sakshi, witness of these emotions. Nothing can disturb me." When you repeat these suggestions of Vichara or Vedantic reflection, the emotions will die by themselves. This is the Jnana-method of driving away the emotions and the strugglings with the mind.

9th December
World: A Wondrous Fair

This world is a big marvellous fair. Father, mother, wife, children, friends, relations are people meeting in a fair. That this is so, there is no doubt. Wealth, honour, titles, status, all pomp and splendour are Maya's jugglery. These are her tempting baits to catch the passionate Jivas. This impure body of flesh, bone and blood is a bubble in the ocean of Samsara. Trust not this body, senses and this tempting world. Through intense Sadhana attain Samadhi and experience your identity with the Infinite Reality and Delight. This experience destroys the longing for fleeting objects of the world. Then there is no more the world of perception. There is Infinite Experience. There is Fullness. There is Perfection. There is Bliss.

10th December
The Upanishadic View of Food

The Upanishads mean by "Food" that which is experienced by consciousness, either directly by itself or indirectly through certain organs. An object that is presented to a conscious subject, is the food of that conscious subject. That which supports, or maintains, or preserves a thing is the food of that thing. In short, food is that, which feeds and sustains individuality. Hence, in the Upanishads, Food is identified with Matter.

11th December
The Method of Vedantic Knowledge

If the body is the soul, your hopes and expectations must increase or decrease, if the energy increases or decreases on account of good health or disease. But this is not so. Even if you are in a dying condition, your hopes do not come to an end. You still hope to get better. You do not like to part with your possessions. This clearly indicates that the soul in the body must be quite distinct from the body itself. It does not come to an end even if the body perishes.

12th December
Uses of Vedanta

Practice of Vedanta will widen your outlook. It will free you from narrow ideas wrong cravings and all kinds of misconceptions. It will enable you to attain Immortal Bliss. Through deep meditation and Samadhi, you will experience Absolute Consciousness. You will be fearless, perfect, full of health and joy. Vedanta elevates the mind to magnanimous heights of Divine Splendour or Brahmanhood; this experience destroys all barriers that separate man from man, brings concord, unruffled peace and harmony to suffering humanity. Vedanta alone can really unite, on the basis of one common Self in all, a Hindu and a Mohammedan, a Catholic and a Protestant, an Irishman and an Englishman, a Jain and a Parsi. A thousand blessings Vedanta holds for every man.

13th December
Influence of the East on the West

The 'Oversoul' of the Western philosophers is the Brahman of the Upanishads, the Atman of the Vedantins. The supreme Soul which is the support of all individuals, is the 'Oversoul'. It is the 'Substance' or the 'Thing-in-itself' of Kant. The essence of

Vedanta has slowly infiltrated into the minds of Western philosophers and they have now accepted the existence of one eternal principle, which is distinct from the body and mind.

The West is irresistibly drawn to the practical philosophy of Vedanta because Vedanta declares that one should not be selfish or attached to any fleeting object, that one should live in the consciousness of the loving brotherhood and unity and of the Self-hood or Atma-hood of the universe, that the Truth of existence is One and indivisible that division or separation, hatred, enmity, quarrel and selfishness are against the Eternal Truth, that the pain of birth and death is caused by desire generated by ignorance of. this great Truth, that the highest state of experience or perfection is Immortal Life or the realisation of Brahman, that everyone is born for this one supreme purpose, that all other duties are only aids or auxiliaries to this great Duty of Self-realisation, that one should perform one's prescribed duties in life with the spirit of non-attachment and of dedication to the Supreme Being, that every aspect of one's life should get consummated in this Supreme Consciousness.

Chapter 34

RELIGION: ITS PHILOSOPHY AND ITS PURPOSES

14th December

Religion and the Modern Temper

Religion is not a dogma or a comfortable fancy or a hobby of a certain group of people. Religion is the expression of the universal impulse which none can resist. Every person thinks differently, and yet, thinks towards the one Supreme Being. Differences are in the roads and the ladders not in the city reached or the roof climbed over. It is the human aspiration, but not the subhuman propensity, that ravages the very values of life through contempt for alien temperaments and hatred towards other inhabitants of the earth, ultimately resulting in religious wars, poverty, grief and restlessness: Modern civilisation despises religion, because it understands by religion an outburst of the irrational spirit. Far from it! Religion is the Light that enlivens the most rational life, the manifestation of the eternal glow of intelligence, that peeps through even the mightiest genius of the world. There can be no civilisation without religion, and there is no worth in religion, if it is destitute of spirituality. There is no Asiatic or American or European, Hindu or Christian or Muslim, but there are sons of God, worshipping Him in the Temple of the Universe.

15th December
The Central Theme of Real Religions

There can be no sense in thinking that one can be happy after denying God, condemning religion, overriding ethics and morality, and sheerly by directing powers against others. The faces drenched by tears, and the stomachs, scorched by hunger, shall bear witness to the criminality of the hands, which have upset the peace of the world. Peace is theirs, who see themselves in all. Those who disrupt the happiness of others cannot be happy. Woe is experienced as a reaction against the woe, that is given to others. Joy is the fruit of joy, given to others. "Do unto others as you wish to be done by."

16th December
A Definition of Real Religion

Religion is faith for knowing and worshipping God. It is not a matter for discussion on a club-table. It is the perception of the true Self. It is the fulfilment of the deepest craving in man. Hold religion as the goal of your life. Live every moment of your life for its realisation. Life without religion is real death.

Real religion is a process of living in God. Religion is not merely a little prayer a man raises when he suffers from severe intestinal colic or chronic dysentery. It is preeminently a life of goodness and service, purity and meditation.

17th December
The Religion of the Heart

The only basis of the true and lasting unity of all humanity is the religion of the heart. Religion of the heart is the religion of love. Men can be unified only, if they are free from jealousy, hatred and petty-mindedness. Purify your heart first. Meet hatred with love, with goodwill.

The essence of religion lies in the immediate experience of the Divine. Man becomes God through discipline, self-restraint, cultivation of fellowship, selfless service, devotion and meditation. Religion is assiduous spiritual practice and Self-realisation.

18th December
The Essential Unity of all Religions

The plurality of "Faiths" will transform itself into one Universal Faith in the eyes of one, who has purified his vision through faith in the fundamentals of his own religion, and who has diligently endeavoured to attain the goal, set before him, by the founder of his own religion. Differences are superficial; the Essential is one and the same in all religions. All the Prophets have alluded to the same God in different terms.

One religion is as good as another. One road to the Supreme is as good as any other road. Cows have different colours, but the colour of milk is one. There are different kinds of roses, but the scent is one. Religion is one, but many are the forms of its practice. Diversity is the order of creation. Religion is no exception to it.

19th December
Wisdom Behind Religious Observances

The Seers of yore have foreseen the inability of the common man to apply himself fully and perfectly to Sadhana for God-realisation. Besides the daily duties, which he has to discharge as a human being, he has also to answer the eternal call of the Divine Truth, which is hidden in him. To this end the Rishis direct man by calling upon him to devote himself fully to such worship on special days like Sivaratri, which are psychologically and astronomically conducive to his spiritual growth.

20th December
Religion Consummates Ethics and Sociology

Where the spirit of selfless service is concerned, religion meets moral philosophy and sociology, for the first posits, that the one Divine Self alone pervades all existence. Hence every piece of service, rendered to others, amounts to benefit, conferred on ourselves. The more this sublime basis of human action is recognised and adopted, the more rapid will be man's evolution towards perfection and divinisation.

Religion is the real foundation of society, the source of all goodness and happiness, the basis of virtue and prosperity of the individual, and through the individual of all humanity. Civilisation, law, order, morality and all that elevates man and gives peace to the world, are the fruits of the practice of religion.

21st December
The Religion of Religions

A universal joy-infusing power of Absolute Religion should take possession of the hearts of all. There is no other purpose in life, if it is not to attain the absolute Perfection, Peace and Joy of the Eternal Being, which all seek, directly or indirectly, and which can be had only, when people understand, that all conceptions of God are aspects of the One Supreme, Immortal, Divine Presence, and that all forms of religion are the aspects of the Great Way to That One Truth. The proper knowledge of this fact shall correct all errors of life and show the method of bringing peace to the world, of making humanity perfect.

22nd December
Unity of Religions

Imagine a pure white canvas, on which is drawn a beautiful evening scenery of a group of pilgrims sitting around a blazing fire by the side of a forest stream. How absurd, would you think, if the water in the picture felt hostile to the fire, drawn thereon. For you know that these two factors are just a trick of a little paint and oil. Beneath it you find the one common canvas, pure and permanent. Rays of one Divine Light! Dwell for ever in the loving awareness of this sweet and glorious unity that throbs in the spiritual heart of the entire mankind. You will be helping invaluable in the noble cause of human solidarity if you will pledge yourself to feel this oneness, assert and manifest this oneness, and propagate and spread this message of unity.

APPENDIX

THE ENDURING BASES FOR INTERNATIONAL IDEALS

23rd December
The Texture of Ancient Indian Society

The ideal of the social ethics of the Gita is Lokasangraha, the well-being and solidarity of the world. This is brought about by each individual through the performance of Svadharma in the spirit of non-attachment and self-surrender. Svadharma aims, at the same time, at Sarvabhutahita or the good of all beings. The fabric of society is to be so constituted, as to aid its members to realise the supreme Ideal of life. As all beings share the one Life which is the whole, and of which they are parts their development lies in being in harmony with that Life. The perfection of the part is in the Unity of the whole. Mutual Love and the execution of duty is loyalty to the whole, is the means to the blessedness of the individual and the society. When each one does his own duty without reluctance or desire in his mind, the welfare of the society is ensured, for wherever action commingles with the knowledge of the Divine Purpose that is behind this visible universe, there shall be prosperity, victory, glory and firm policy.

24th December
India and Modern Civilisation

Modern civilisation has not cared to understand the fundamental meaning of life, but it is satisfied with mere floating upon the perceptible surface of the physical existence. The present-day science, however penetrating it may be, is after all an investigation into the world of common experience in the waking state; it has discarded the deep significance of the changes that man undergoes in the states of his deeper life. India has got the credit of having found the very root of life, and of having discovered the Permanent Ground upon which is played the drama of life. If there is anything valuable in life as a whole, it is the knowledge of the solution of the apparent riddle of existence, and this is the glorious heritage of India.

25th December
Individual Good and the Welfare of Mankind

The superstructure of national, social and domestic life can be erected in a manner that will strike the best balance between the individual good and the welfare of mankind in general. Selflessness is a virtue that blends individual good with the welfare of society. On this loom of selflessness, individual good and the good of society become the warp and woof, producing the fabric of a commonwealth in which all the individuals are happy, prosperous and peaceful; the fabric of a civilisation which is characterised by peace and progress all round. Let us vigorously work towards this peak of achievement.

26th December
Practicable Ideals for the Nations

The aim of nations should be to direct their power towards the transformation of the hearts of the people from the subhuman and the weak human nature into the rightly human and divine natures through right government, right education and insistence on right living, based on perfect Truth. This shall effect the great renaissance for the healthy and peaceful life of all on earth, and also for the Eternal Life transcending the earthly life.

Man cannot discard material prosperity, nor can he ignore spiritual refinement. Either he effects this balance between material prosperity and spiritual progress, and thereby ensures peace and welfare, or he destroys himself through the worship of the deities of materialism, by their subservient genie, the weapons of destruction.

27th December
Beneath the Civilised Barbarism

It is worth remembering that the universal degeneration of the human character and unrestricted play of baser passions in the individual and social life, is at the root of each repeated wave of scientific and civilised barbarism that sweeps over the world time and again. Uncontrolled human passion is certain to plunge the nations into savage warfare in the future also. A living faith in spiritual values and earnest practical religion seem to be the one hope if mankind is to live. The refinement, ennobling and sublimation of human passion and desire are the special function and purpose of true Religion. The dictates of elementary logic and rationality clearly direct that to rescue humanity from the present and safeguard it in the future, the right way is to recognise the important role of Ethics.

28th December

Towards One World

Behold the Self in all; he who knows that the same life, that throbs in the innermost recess of his heart, indwells others too, dares not harm anybody; for, if he does harm anybody, he harms but himself. In a fray one might injure his brother. But under no circumstances would one wish to hurt himself. When a person on to a robbery feels that he is to rob his own hard-earned property, when one assigned to murder another person, belonging to a rival community, feels that he is but to murder himself, when a nation set out to aggrandise another nation feels, that it is actually exploiting and slaughtering its own people only then will the inner call to desist from these savage acts come. This spirit of oneness must be cultivated and intensified in every human being.

29th December

Raison d'être of All Relationship

If family or society or nation is understood as a means to separate one from another, however large the scope of its inclusion of human beings may be, such a family, such a society, such a nation cannot triumph. All relationship is expected to end in the absolute unity of existence, excluding nothing from itself. This goal of life should be borne in mind in the process of our daily activities, if our actions are to be free from selfishness, if our actions are to be at-one with the universal movement of Nature. Life is a divine worship. The proper conduct of family, the administration of the country and the society, is a part of the Universal Government which looks at the entirety of beings with a strict impartial eye.

30th December

Reconciliation of Science and Technology With the Peace-giving Culture

What is wrong with science? What is defective in technology? The implements that help man cook his food could kill him if they are misused and abused. Electricity has come to be the very "breath of life." But, then, it should be used with caution and with the sole aim of subserving man's selfless longing to serve his fellowmen. Science is not the enemy of culture; science and culture are sisters. They can live together amicably and help make the house (the world) a paradise if there is the bond of real love uniting their hearts. Once the basic ideology if accepted and implemented, why should science itself not be elevated to the grand status of a cultural institution? Technology will be a branch of national culture. They can promote the spiritual welfare of man, enrich his heart, broaden his outlook and enlighten his soul, as profoundly as any other branch of culture can.

Not because there is anything diabolical in scientific advance itself does culture look upon it with an eye of suspicion and dread. But, it is because the canker of uncultured, baser, animal passions eats the very vitals of Man in whose erring hand science serves as the best suicidal agency. If culture enters the heart of man, if cultural institutions receive the rightful place of honour in all Plans and Schemes of nation-building the world over, then science itself will promote culture!

31st December

The Ultimate Message—Realise: "I am the Immortal Self"

BROTHER! Courage is your birthright, not fear. Peace is your divine heritage, not restlessness; Immortality, not mortality; Strength, not weakness; Health, not disease; Bliss, not sorrow; Knowledge, not ignorance.

Thou art Divine. Live up to it. Feel and realise thy divine nature. Thou art the master of thy own destiny. Do not be discouraged when sorrows, difficulties and tribulations manifest in the daily battle of life. Draw up courage and spiritual strength from within. There is a vast inexhaustible magazine of power and knowledge within. Tap it. Plunge yourself in the sacred waters of Immortality. You will be quite refreshed, renovated and vivified when you go to the divine source and realise: "I am the Immortal Self."

Rely on your own Self. Be not a slave. You are the Immortal Self. Destroy inferiority complex. Draw power, courage, strength from within. Be free. Believe not in any dogmas. Have no blind faith. Accept nothing except after reasoning out carefully. Never be carried away by the blind surging emotions. Subdue them. Be not intolerant. Expand. Constant meditation on your inner Immortal Self, is the master-key to open the realms of Knowledge. Your essential nature is Sat-Chit-Ananda, Existence-Knowledge-Bliss-Absolute. The outer cloak, this mortal physical body is an illusory Mayaic production. You are the sexless Self, the King of kings; you are Immortal and Infinite. Feel. Assert. Recognise. Realise, not from tomorrow, but right now. O Blessed one! Thou art Immortal!